Fought

Served

Abandoned

Vietnam War Was Necessary

We Were Lied To

Stories of My Vietnam War Experiences

By

Randy Tompkins

Fought, Served, Abandoned
All Rights Reserved.
Copyright © 2019 Randy Tompkins
v2.0

The opinions expressed in this manuscript are solely the opinions of the author and do not represent the opinions or thoughts of the publisher. The author has represented and warranted full ownership and/or legal right to publish all the materials in this book.

This book may not be reproduced, transmitted, or stored in whole or in part by any means, including graphic, electronic, or mechanical without the express written consent of the publisher except in the case of brief quotations embodied in critical articles and reviews.

Outskirts Press, Inc.
http://www.outskirtspress.com

ISBN: 978-1-9772-1292-4

Cover Photo © 2019 Randy Tompkins. All rights reserved - used with permission.

Outskirts Press and the "OP" logo are trademarks belonging to Outskirts Press, Inc.

PRINTED IN THE UNITED STATES OF AMERICA

TABLE OF CONTENTS

Disclaimer.. i
Purpose for this Book... 1
Vietnam - First Enemy Attack When
   I First Arrived in Vietnam 18
Vietnam - What My Job and Responsibilities Were 22
Vietnam - M-60 Machine Gun – My Weapon Of Death....... 25
Vietnam Experience of Blowing Up One of Our Helicopters 28
After Vietnam War Experiences... 32
My Vietnam Experience with a Twelve Hole Latrine (toilet).. 38
Vietnam – Wounded Buttocks Story.. 41
Vietnam – The Zippo Cigarette Lighter.................................... 47
Vietnam – Discovering One of My Unique Abilities 49
My Experiences on R&R from Vietnam in Thailand 52
My Vietnam Rat Experience 55
Vietnam Fragment Grenade Story 57
Vietnam – Training to Survive 62
Vietnam – A Little, Ornery, Wild Side 69
Vietnam – My Experiences with Racial Tension 74
Vietnam – Women and Children Enemy Soldiers................... 79
Vietnam – Relationships with the Guys! 83
Vietnam – Anti-war Demonstrations 89
Vietnam – Thou Shall Not Kill! Am I Condemned?............... 93
Vietnam – Tanks (and Tankers) Were A

Vietnam War Blessing	97
Vietnam – The Ho Chi Minh Trail	102
Vietnam – Puff, the Magic Dragon	105
Vietnam – The Air Force Had It Made!	108
Vietnam Entertainment – Vietnamese Rock Band and Go-Go Girls	113
Vietnam - Broken Heart	117
Vietnam – The Grunt's War	120
Vietnam – Pain in the Butt Sappers!	127
Vietnam – The Saga of Hamburger Hill	136
Vietnam News – The Stars and Stripes Newspaper	143
Vietnam – General VoNguyen Giap – North Vietnamese General	146
The Vietnam War Still Raging For Vietnam Veterans 40 years Later	148
Vietnam - When I Just About Became a POW (prisoner of war)	153
Vietnam – Hanoi Jane, a Traitor	157
Vietnam - The Emotions of Arriving Home Coming From the Vietnam War	158
Something I Discovered About America And Vietnam Veterans	163
About the Author	166
Acknowledgments	168
Contact Information	170

Scout Patch Randy Wore On His Shirts In Vietnam

I wore this patch on my flight shirt and regular jungle fatigues. This patch had a $1000 reward on it. If an enemy soldier, NVA or VC, killed or captured anyone wearing this patch, they were awarded $1000. That made that soldier very wealthy. I never wore this patch when I sneaked through the perimeter wire to go to the village. I wore it everywhere else 24/7. It garnered lots of respect among the American soldiers. We received a lot of privileges as a result of this patch. I was very proud to wear it.

Patch Worn By Cobra Gunship Pilots

Patch Worn By Slick Helicopter Pilots, Crew Chiefs, and Slick Gunners

Scout LOACH Maintenance Personnel Patch

Patch Worn By Some Cobra Gunship Pilots

Patch Worn By The Aero Rifle Patrol

DISCLAIMER

I AM GIVING a disclaimer on the contents of this book. I buried my experiences in the Vietnam War so deep inside my soul, I have forgotten some names, some places, and some details. I still remember enough for the pain to still hurt badly and write good stories. I shoved all these memories into a deep, dark place to finally bring them to the surface so I can be healed!

I have stated on the cover of this book, being in South Vietnam was necessary. That was to protect our national interests. This is explained later. The research I did in the library at Black Hills State College (now University) in 1966 – 1967 shaped my opinion. You can use the Yahoo search engine to find the same information I found back over fifty years ago. No computers were available back then, only magazines and books. The mainstream news media mentioned not one of my findings anywhere that I read or heard, newspaper or TV. Their reporting was continually biased in my opinion. The news media wanted the United States out of Vietnam. Because of the omission of this information, available to anyone who really wanted to know what I wanted to know, I personally feel we, the American people, were lied to about the Vietnam War and its purpose. I have always been taught that omission of facts that can affect the truth is the same as lying. This is my opinion. I take ownership of it.

The pictures used in this book were obtained from friends and fellow platoon members. I wanted to use internet pictures, but my publisher said that was not allowed unless I received permission to use them. Getting permission is almost impossible. I want to use pictures to give the reader a better visual of my stories so the reader can connect easier. The pictures are at the end of each story that have them. I have not used names of the people I served with because I do not have permission to do so and, frankly, I do not remember some of their names. This book is written in generalities. If you are looking for detailed, technical specifics, this is not the book for you. What you are getting are stories told from the heart and with enough details, so the story is personal. Hopefully, you will feel as if you are right there with me! That is my goal! I want my fellow Vietnam War veterans to be back in Vietnam with me. I want them to feel, experience the pain, cry, and start on the road to healing. It amazes me, to this day, how may Vietnam War veterans still suffer from Post Traumatic Stress Disorder (PTSD) after fifty years or more of having to deal with such a disorder. The Veterans Administration is finally diagnosing PTSD in many of the Vietnam War veterans helping these brave heroes, who were shunned and scorned by America upon arriving home, to be healed. Blessed be my war brothers!

PURPOSE FOR THIS BOOK

ON NOVEMBER 16, 2018 and November 17, 2018, I had one of the most exhilarating, uplifting, healing experiences of my life as a Vietnam War veteran! My oldest brother, Larry Tompkins, my wife, Sally, and I made the trip to Timber Lake, South Dakota. Larry graduated from Timber Lake High School in 1961. I graduated from there in 1964. We were invited for a meet and greet by Kathy Nelson, publisher of the Timber Lake Topic, the local newspaper. The Timber Lake Topic had been running a series of stories written by me of my experiences in the Vietnam War. Kathy invited us because the readers of the Timber Lake Topic were really interested in the series. They wanted to meet me and my family, some for the first time. Many of the local Vietnam veterans showed great interest. Kathy mentioned I had become somewhat of a local celebrity. I think Kathy was working me a little, stroking my ego! It worked! I accepted her invitation.

This whole saga started on July 4, 2018. For some reason, I felt inspired to dig out the memorabilia I had of the Vietnam War. Why? I do not know, but I did it! I felt I needed to share these things with my family. No one had seen any of this stuff, except my son, Heath, as a young boy. Even my wife had not seen any of it. I took my memorabilia with me to our family reunion August 10, 2018, held in Minneapolis, Minnesota, to share with my brothers and sisters. Whoa! Did that ever let the bees out of the hive! My family was really upset with me that I had not shown them any of my Vietnam War stuff or shared my Vietnam War stories prior to that time, especially before my dad died. My youngest sister, Lois, was really close to my dad, being the baby in the family. She was so angry with me she started crying. My dad always wanted to know what happened to me in Vietnam. Lois was in tears when she asked me why I had not shared any of my Vietnam experiences with them before. With deep, gut wrenching emotion and a lump in my throat, I said, "I couldn't! I just couldn't!" She and the rest of the family made me promise I would write down my Vietnam War experiences and email them to each family. At the family reunion I sat down with my brother Larry's grand children to tell them a couple of stories about their grandpa. I felt it was important they knew these stories as part of their family history. During this process, their dad Scott, my nephew, asked me to share a Vietnam War story with them. They were mesmerized as I steered them through one of my experiences. They really enjoyed the story, asked me some questions, and processed what I had told them. I went into enough details, emotion, and feelings so they could really visualize what it was like for Vietnam War veterans in Vietnam.

Because I am a man of my word, I started writing stories about my experiences in Vietnam. It was painfully difficult at first. I was digging deep into my pain storage bin where I had stored all my emotions, pain, and feelings about the Vietnam War. I cried a lot. A whole lot. Each time I wrote a story another one would come to my mind and I would cry as I wrote. The pain and the emotions of the war and what I had experienced because of the negative reception I received when I arrived home, rose to the surface all over again. Some Vietnam veterans had rotten tomatoes and other things thrown at them while on their way home in uniform. It got to the point where our returning Vietnam War brothers were advised not to wear their uniforms home because of the unpopularity of the war and all the protesters at the airports. I just did not know whether I could go through all the pain again and again. Then, I noticed something positive. I was starting to heal! It was as if I were in counseling with a psychiatrist and that psychiatrist was pulling all these deep and painful feelings out into the open. I wore my uniform home so I could get the military discount plane ticket. A soldier had to wear their uniform to get the discount. The homecoming reception by the community where my family lived was not good. I did not live there very long (two years) moving there after high school graduation. It was just long enough to get drafted. No one wanted to have anything to do with me. So, I left burying all the memories, pain, sorrow, names, places way deep into a dark place never to be thought of again. If someone asked me a question about my experiences in Vietnam, I would give them an answer, but a very short, shallow one. I realized later, after reading other Vietnam War veterans experiences, my old friends and people in town where my family lived, were afraid of me. I am having a little trouble grasping that, but I guess I cannot blame them. The news media did not paint a pretty picture of Vietnam veterans.

I decided, if I am going to do all this work to write these stories, I might as well post them on Facebook along with pictures to support the story! I was not much of a Facebook user. I had never posted anything on Facebook at all. I did not have a very good understanding of how it all worked! As I posted my Vietnam stories, the number of responses, shares, people who reacted, and those who liked were shocking to me. Some of the posts were responded to in under a minute of the post. The love, encouragement, and "thank you for your service" was overwhelming! I was flabbergasted! Dumbfounded! Astonished! I was even encouraged to write a book. What the heck! I can't write a book! I am just telling a few stories. However, my decision was to tell every story from the heart. I wanted the reader to feel they were right there with me. Evidently, I must have accomplished that by the comments I received. Oh, by the way! I want you Vietnam brothers to know, they all welcomed me home and thanked me for my service to my country. That is something I had never received for over forty years, except for one time when my wife and I were attending the night presentation at Mt. Rushmore in the Black Hills of South Dakota where they light the faces up!

Before the presentation, they invite all the veterans and military personnel down front to the stage to receive recognition and appreciation applause from the audience. On this particular night they invited wives also. Sally and I walked down to the stage. I was the first one to be handed the microphone. They wanted us to state our name, where we were from, what branch of service we served in, and what war we had fought in. I stated my name, Randy Tompkins from Zanesville, Ohio, but originally from South Dakota, I was drafted into the Army, and I served in Vietnam for a year and a half being awarded the Purple Heart. Next to me was a group of young Army officers, male and female, who were in the Black Hills for special training. They introduced themselves along with approximately fifty other veterans and military personnel.

After the ceremony and lighting of the faces was over, on the way out my wife had to use the rest room. As I was waiting outside the rest room area, this group of young Army officers approached me. One of them said, "You served in Vietnam, did you?" I said, "Yes! I was there for a year and a half!" Then he said, "I want to thank you for your service in Vietnam. If it was not for what you guys did in Vietnam, we would not be as far as we are in war strategy and training. Thank you so much!" He shook my hand as did the rest of the group of about a dozen soldiers. Each sincerely thanked me for serving in Vietnam. I could hardly say thank you because of the lump I had in my throat. That was the first thank you, ever, for my service in Vietnam. It was an emotional experience for me and still is when I think about it.

I graduated with Pat (Humann) Kjellsen, who was reading my Vietnam stories on Facebook. She said she was really enjoying my stories and so did others whom she was acquainted with. She encouraged me to let the Timber Lake Topic (local newspaper) publish my stories. She not only told me the communities the paper served, but also, other Vietnam veterans would enjoy my writings of my Vietnam War experiences. I contacted Kathy Nelson, the Timber Lake Topic publisher, to see if she would be interested. She responded with an enthusiastic "YES!" I discovered later that Kathy Nelson has the energy of the "Energizer Bunny," as she is the pulse and heartbeat of the community. She and her staff took these stories and made them into a phenomenal series. Even I got excited when I read them in the newspaper. And I wrote them!

People far and wide, who still are connected to the Timber Lake community by subscribing to the Timber Lake Topic, started contacting me by email, Facebook, and phone. I am so humbled, grateful, appreciative, and thankful for all the love, encouragement, healing, and inspiration I have received from everyone.

All of this has contributed to my "happy place!"

Friday night, November 16, 2018, at the meet and greet in the Timber Lake Museum, I started my presentation at 7 PM. I introduced myself, told a few family stories, and presented my Vietnam experiences. Everyone was so attentive and zeroed in on what I had to say. Their meaningful questions as well as comments made by some of the Vietnam veterans in attendance added immensely to the quality of the gathering. After starting at 7 PM, the next thing I know it is 10:30 PM and we had not had a break or refreshments yet. Everyone was so engrossed in what was going on, we lost track of time. My brother, Larry, said something that it was 10:15 PM, but I did not hear him. Attendees said they did not realize that much time had passed. During refreshments Larry, Sally, and I really had an opportunity to connect with so many people, old acquaintances and new ones. It was so fulfilling and joyful! I encouraged all the Vietnam brothers of mine, in attendance, to please write down their stories and do it from the heart. Please do not take this important history to the grave with you. Your family and friends deserve to know what happened to you in the Vietnam War. Leave something meaningful for your kids, grandkids, great-grand kids, on down the ancestral line. Our posterity and descendants want to know about us, as I want to know my ancestors as I do genealogy.

Yes! You will cry a lot and it will be extremely painful, but you will heal. Your soul will not be pained anymore.

Saturday morning, November 17, 2018, of the meet and greet started off with coffee and donuts along with a whole lot of fellowship. I felt as if I were at a church meeting without the minister present, there was so much joy and love being passed around. Some of the attendees returned from the night before presentation to hear more. Again, the presentation went a long time because of the interest. Some of my Vietnam brothers shared some very personal stories of their own. Maybe my pleas are starting to reach these guys. The need to just write their stories down is paramount.

Larry, Sally, and I were talking on the way back home. We could not believe how unbelievable of a time we had. All of us commented on how much love we received, how welcomed we felt, and how organized everything was. Kathy Nelson is one heck of an organizer and a very good detail person. On top of that, she researched things that Larry and I could not give good details about when we lived in Timber Lake. She was also taking notes and pictures throughout the whole meet and greet. She probably has record of all the tissues that may have been used. I know I was getting emotional several times throughout the meeting.

Later Kathy and I discussed a possible book. It was the farthest thing from my mind even after I was encouraged to write a book. Now that I am aware of all the Vietnam veterans my stories are helping, that is my motivation to write this book. I want to help my fellow Vietnam War brothers to come out of the Vietnam War closet. The pain and suffering have been festering deep inside each of my war brothers long enough. I have reached a point I enjoy crying. I always thought it was a woman thing or a child thing. Not anymore! My sister, Lois, called me to ask if she could forward all my stories (35 of them) to a friend of hers whose brother served in Vietnam and still had issues that affected his wellbeing in life. I said, "Of course! I am posting them on Facebook. All the world can read them!" She forwarded them onto her friend. Her friend contacted Lois again to sincerely and emotionally thank me. Lois' friend gave all the stories to her brother who read them all. The flood gates broke! My sister's friend said she now has her brother back. That is humbling and gives hope that I can help others.

After writing 35 stories of my experiences in the Vietnam War and traveling from Zanesville, Ohio to Timber Lake, South Dakota, I have come to an interesting conclusion. My Vietnam War brothers and I arrived home to the United States and our home towns with excitement. We were not welcomed nor treated kindly. We received nothing! It was hurtful and painful as well as discouraging. As a result of the response to my stories and the Meet and Greet, I have reached this conclusion. America wants to repent of how the Vietnam War veterans were treated. I truly feel they realized they messed up and want to make things right. People are not afraid of us anymore. People are so interested in what each of us Vietnam War veterans went through, what we felt, and how we dealt with a war that was so unpopular. This was a war most of us did not volunteer for. Many of us were drafted. We did what we did because of our love of America and our families! We swore to uphold and defend the Constitution of the United States against all enemies, foreign and domestic so help me God! We swore to honor our flag and the national anthem! We did our duty expecting nothing. When we arrived home, nothing is what we got!

Many comments are made, "I did not know that! That is so interesting!" I have received hundreds of "I want to thank you" and "We love you" from folks from all walks of life and scores of veterans! Damn, that feels good! In discussing what I have been experiencing sharing my Vietnam War experiences with my VA Primary Care Provider doctor and how it has helped other war veterans, she reacted as if a light came on in her brain. Seventy percent of her patients are Vietnam War veterans. She told me she was going to encourage these patients to sit down and write about their war experiences. I think that is good advice for any war veteran whether they fought in World War II, Korea, Desert Storm, Iraq, or Afghanistan. I have personally found that bringing all of this up to the surface, facing it, recognizing what I did was right, lifts the burden from the soul. America now wants to give each of us Vietnam War veterans love, thanks, and appreciation. How do I know that? That is what I have received as a result of sharing my Vietnam stories. It has been one of the wisest, smartest, and most enlightening decisions I have made in my life! It has also been one of great healing, something that was needed to bring out those deepest, hidden, pains of war and turn them into something I now can be proud of. Before, I did not feel proud of my service in Vietnam at all! Now I do, thanks to caring friends (old and new), family, veterans, and fellow Vietnam War brothers.

I say to you my brothers! Come out of the Vietnam War closet, share your stories in writing with family and friends, let the process have its healing ways (yes, you will cry a lot and fight the pain that comes) so you too can feel proud of having served in the Vietnam War. Please do not take this history to the grave with you! Write it down!

I want to share with you why I felt we should be fighting in Vietnam. You may think, "What the hell is he talking about! No way!" Hear me out! I want you to be proud of serving in Vietnam as I have come to be proud. Your fighting was not in vain!

I was attending college at Black Hills State College (now University) in Spearfish, South Dakota. I was taking a speech class. For the final grade we had to give a 15 to 20-minute speech. I wanted to get an "A." I wanted to speak on something that would have a profound impact on the audience. The news media (TV and newspapers) was constantly reporting on protests and negatively reporting on the Vietnam War trying to influence the United States leaders to get us out of Vietnam. I kept thinking in my mind there had to be a logical reason why President John F. Kennedy sent troops there in the first place. I saw him as a wise President who would not do something unless it was highly important. So, instead of focusing on why we should not be fighting in Vietnam, I decided to focus on why we should be fighting in Vietnam. I went to the college library to research important information about our troops being sent to Vietnam to fight. What I found was shocking and a big surprise to me. I heard nothing what I discovered being reported in the main stream media!

I found the second most used shipping lane in the world went around the southern tip of South Vietnam in the China Sea. Whoever controlled South Vietnam would control a major commercial water way which would affect world commerce. Another thing I discovered is that South Vietnam was rich (and still is) in minerals and ores...uranium, gold, silver, iron, oil, gas, timber, useful medicinal plants, etc. Russia and China were financing the North Vietnamese in their war effort. All three countries are communist countries. Russia and China wanted control of South Vietnam. South Vietnam asked President Kennedy for help! In his wisdom I feel President Kennedy thought the same thing I did. If Russia and China gained control of South Vietnam, they could use all these resources against us. The Cold War with Russia was still in its heightened years. It made sense to me for us to be fighting in Vietnam. I would rather fight there than here at home where our families would be harmed. We needed to be in South Vietnam protecting our national interests. By the way, I received my "A." I had several classmates come up to thank me for answering the questions they had similar to mine. Even the professor, somewhat of a liberal, said I had given her a lot to think about. She thanked me.

The politicians never attempted to explain any of this to us. I really believe if America knew all of this, the draft would not have been necessary. Thousands would have volunteered to defend our country because of their love of country and patriotism. They would have wanted to protect the future of America just as I wanted to. I was drafted, but I was willing to serve in Vietnam. Even though North Vietnam took over South Vietnam after the U.S. Military pulled out, the 1975 Paris Treaty kept Russia and China out of Vietnam. All those natural resources are still untouched. In fact, Vietnam is beginning to open up to tourism, factories, and other capital enterprises. I am occasionally seeing things made in Vietnam here in America. Vietnam leaders finally realized they could become a wealthy nation with our help. The Vietnamese living in the large cities in South Vietnam during the war experienced a higher standard of living and increased wealth as a result of the presence of the U.S. Military. One can get information on the minerals and natural resources in South Vietnam from FactsandDetails.com.

So, I went to Vietnam with a little bit of a different attitude than most of our soldiers who did not have the same knowledge I had! I was 24 years old, had been away from home, and had already experienced some homesickness. Many of the troops sent to Vietnam were 18-19-year-old kids who had never been away from home. Age, lack of knowledge, homesickness, and loneliness along with a whole bunch of fear contributed to the mindset of rejected, returning soldiers deep, deep in pain. Let's rise above it, brothers! Write your stories down, cry, and heal! I promise you it works! My war soul has been healed!

That is why I am writing this book. It is not written in chronological order. It is written by stories with supporting pictures to help the reader feel they are there with me. Please enjoy the read! Thanks a million!

Orders For The Purple Heart Metal Award

DEPARTMENT OF THE ARMY
HEADQUARTERS 17TH AVIATION GROUP (COMBAT)
APO San Francisco 96316
"FREEDOM'S EAGLES"

GENERAL ORDERS 6 October 1971
NUMBER   149

TC 439. The following AWARDS are announced.

SHEEHAN JOHN F ████████ WO1 100E C Trp 7/17th CAV (WAZNCO) APO 96226 AV
Date of action: 25 Feb 71 VOCO 17th CAG date cfm

GENSINGER DAVID R ████████ SSG 11D40 D Trp 1/10 CAV (WAKEDO) APO 96226
Date of action: 4 Sep 71 VOCO 17th CAG date cfm

HOOVER BRIAN M ████████ SP4 11B2P D Trp 1/10 (WAKEDO) APO 96226
Date of action: 5 Jun 71 VOCO 17th CAG date cfm

TOMPKINS RANDALL L ████████ SF5 45J20 D Trp 1/10 CAV (WAKEDO) APO 96226
Date of action: 10 Aug 71 VOCO 17th CAG date cfm

EDWARDS JAMES H III ████████ SP4 67N2F 192nd AHC (WDUYAA) APO 96377
Date of action: 14 Aug 71 VOCO 17th CAG date cfm

SHRIVER CHARLES L ████████ SP4 67N2A 192nd AHC (WDUYAA) APO 96377
Date of action: 24 Jun 71 VOCO 17th CAG date cfm

BALLEW PETER J ████████ SP5 45M20 192nd AHC (WDUYAA) APO 96377
Date of action: 25 Aug 71 VOCO 17th CAG date cfm

LINVILLE LESTER R ████████ SP4 67N2F 192nd AHC (WDUYAA) APO 96377
Date of action: 5 Sep 71 VOCO 17th CAG date cfm

KING LARRY D ████████ CPT 1981 192nd AHC (WDUYAA) APO 96377 IN
Date of action: 10 Aug 71 VOCO 17th CAG date cfm

NEU GERALD J ████████ SP4 11B2P Co C 75th Inf (WG74AA) APO 96316
Date of action: 23 Sep 71 VOCO 17th CAG date cfm

FULLER JIM M ████████ SP4 11B2P Co C 75th Inf (WG74AA) APO 96316
Date of action: 8 Sep 71 VOCO 17th CAG date cfm

WILLIAMS JOSEPH L ████████ SP4 Co C 75th Inf (WG74AA) APO 96316
Date of action: 14 Jul 71 VOCO 17th CAG date cfm

Awarded: Purple Heart (1st Award)
Theater: Republic of Vietnam
Authority: By direction of the President UP AR 672-5.
Reason: For wounds received in connection with military operations against a hostile force.

Purple Heart Metal

Distinguished Flying Cross Medal

Orders Awarding Me the Distinguished Flying Cross and the Reason

DEPARTMENT OF THE ARMY
HEADQUARTERS, 1ST AVIATION BRIGADE
APO San Francisco 96384

"NGUY HIEM"

GENERAL ORDERS
NUMBER 1747

15 June 1972

AWARD OF THE DISTINGUISHED FLYING CROSS

TC 439. The following AWARD is announced.

TOMPKINS, RANDALL L. ~~[redacted]~~ SP5 67N20 D Trp, 1/10th Air Cav (HAKEDO)
APO 96226

Awarded: Distinguished Flying Cross
Date of service: 10 August 1971
Theater: Republic of Vietnam
Authority: By direction of the President under the provisions of the Act of Congress, approved 2 July 1962, AR 672-5-1 and USARV Supplement 1 to AR 672-5-1, dated 10 August 1970.
Reason: For heroism while participating in aerial flight evidenced by voluntary actions above and beyond the call of duty: Specialist Five Tompkins distinguished himself by exceptionally valorous actions during a reconnaissance mission in the area due north of fire support base Buffalo early in the evening while on visual reconnaissance, the lead scout ship received fire. Specialist Tompkins returned fire and directed his pilot to a position where he could place a smoke grenade to mark the area for a gunship attack. On a second reconnaissance of the area they again received hostile fire and he again laid down suppresive fire covering his ship and his sister ship. At this time all parties returned to An-Khe to refuel and rearm. Upon return, the enemy launched an ambush upon the scout team with automatic weapons. Specialist Tompkins remained calm and efficient while he returned suppressive fire. After the action, it was noted that he had been wounded seriously. Despite this, he remained at station firing at the enemy until the gunships were inbound with a confirmed target. His actions were in keeping with the highest military traditions and reflect great credit upon himself, his unit, and the United States Army.

FOR THE COMMANDER:

OFFICIAL:

H. W. Ide

H. W. IDE
CW2, USA
Asst AG

ROBLEY W. DAVIS, Jr.
Lieutenant Colonel, GS
Chief of Staff

Reason for this award is enlarged on the next page.

plement 1 to AR 0/2-)-1, dated 10 August 19/--

Reason: For heroism while participating in aerial flight evidenced by voluntary actions above and beyond the call of duty: Specialist Five Tompkins distinguished himself by exceptionally valorous actions during a reconnaissance mission in the area due north of fire support base Buffalo early in the evening while on visual reconnaissance, the lead scout ship received fire. Specialist Tompkins returned fire and directed his pilot to a position where he could place a smoke grenade to mark the area for a gunship attack. On a second reconnaissance of the area they again received hostile fire and he again laid down suppresive fire covering his ship and his sister ship. At this time all parties returned to An-Khe to refuel and rearm. Upon return, the enemy launched an ambush upon the scout team with automatic weapons. Specialist Tompkins remained calm and efficient while he returned suppressive fire. After the action, it was noted that he had been wounded seriously. Despite this, he remained at station firing at the enemy until the gunships were inbound with a confirmed target. His actions were in keeping with the highest military traditions and reflect great credit upon himself, his unit, and the United States Army.

Picture of Me in Vietnam (25 years old)

Randy Tompkins in Vietnam

VIETNAM - FIRST ENEMY ATTACK WHEN I FIRST ARRIVED IN VIETNAM

WHEN FINISHING MY 30 day leave prior to going to Vietnam, I had to report to McCord Air Force Base outside of the Seattle/Tacoma, Washington area. We boarded our plane bound for Cam Ranh Bay, South Vietnam around 2 A.M. in the morning on July 4, 1970. I had just turned 24 years old on July 2, 1970. It was an outdoor boarding situation, so we walked in single file in a long line to go up the steps to the get inside the large passenger plane owned by Tiger Airlines. They contracted to fly soldiers to Vietnam. As we were walking to our plane, another plane had just landed unloading soldiers returning from Vietnam with us passing each other. Naturally, it was normal for us to ask where they were coming from and how safe it was. It was natural for them to ask us where we were going. They told us they had come from Cam Ranh Bay, it was safe, and had not been attacked for over two years. That was very comforting to us, not knowing the unknown. That made me feel so good I convinced all the female Flight Attendants to give me a kiss hello and a kiss goodbye as I got off the plane. I convinced them I would not see another American girl for a long time. I needed something to help me remember our beautiful women and give me hope that I would be returning home. I had a lot of fun with them.

We landed in Anchorage, Alaska, Tokyo, Japan, and then Cam

Ranh Bay, South Vietnam July 5,1970. We were bused to a holding company until we could receive our orders for our permanent duty station. We were issued M-16 automatic rifles along with ammunition the first day. Everyone had one. I found out later Cam Ranh Bay was used for in-country R&R (Rest and Recuperation).

The second night we were in Cam Ranh Bay we started receiving incoming enemy mortars. The warning sirens started wailing, chaos was everywhere, and everyone was heading for an underground bunker for safety. As I stepped out of the two-story hooch I was living in, M-16 rounds were going off all around me. Scared, inexperienced, F***ing New Guys (FNG's were what new guys fresh in country were called and I was one) were accidentally firing off their M-16's. This scared the crap out of me. When one is scared or high on adrenaline (natural body stimulator), the butt hole puckers up! This is called pucker factor! The more scared a person is or the higher one is on adrenaline the greater the pucker factor. My pucker factor was high! I looked for a safe area to get away from all of this. I climbed up onto the roof of the two -tory hooch I was living in to watch the spectacular event from a good vantage point to stay out of the way of idiots firing off their weapons. Off in a short distance enemy mortar rounds were destroying our ammunition dump. It looked like a huge 4th of July celebration. In about ten minutes I was joined by another guy who felt the same way I did about the ridiculous panic that was going on. This all lasted about a half hour. So much for not being attacked by the enemy for over two years.

We were held in this holding company for two weeks before being shipped out to our permanent combat units. Every morning a Sergeant would come in around 5:30 a.m. to get everyone up to assign them to some kind of duty detail. Some would have to pull KP (Kitchen Police-wash dishes), some would be placed on guard duty, and others would be put on clean up details. I hated all of them. I would get up about 5 a.m., walk the mile to the beach, and lay in the sun all day until dinner time. That was my first experience lying in the sun bathing on a beach, being from South Dakota. No beach front property in South Dakota! I only ate one meal per day, but it got me out of all the crap detail work.

One evening while walking to dinner, I passed a Second Lieutenant officer (shave tail). I did not salute. He stopped me, chewed me up one side, and down the other. I apologized and told him I would salute him whenever I passed him so the enemy snipers would know who the officers were. He was an FNG and had not been told that enemy snipers loved to take out our officers. He dismissed me and said, "Never mind!" When I arrived at Phan Thiet, south of Cam Ranh Bay, my permanent duty station, I was asked how long I had been in country. I said I had only been in country two weeks. They thought I was lying to them because I had such a dark tan, which other FNG's did not have. I enjoyed a two-week vacation before I even started.

Later in September 1970, I was medivaced to Okinawa Camp Kue Army Hospital for two and half months. When I was sent back to Vietnam, I was sent to An Khe located in the Central Highlands of South Vietnam.

Vietnam - Captured Enemy Mortar Launcher

VIETNAM - WHAT MY JOB AND RESPONSIBILITIES WERE

MY TRAINING BEFORE I arrived in South Vietnam was Aircraft Armament Repair. This job was repairing and installing weapon systems as well as re-arming the Cobra Gunship. The Cobra Gunship was armed with rocket pods on each side and two miniguns in the turret under the nose of the Cobra. Sometimes a grenade launcher replaced one of the miniguns. Miniguns had six barrels that put out 6000 rounds per minute. Firing their miniguns and rockets reduced an enemy fighting force to rubble in seconds! The enemy ran away as fast as they could from the Cobra Gunships! When I arrived in Phan Thiet, I was assigned as a crew chief on a Cobra Gunship. I had no training on the mechanical care of a helicopter. I was told I would learn quickly. My platoon sergeant gave me a crash course on my responsibilities. I have always been somewhat mechanically inclined since I was raised on a 3000-acre ranch. I had to learn to repair tractors, pickups, trucks, and equipment. So, I had some turn-the-wrench experience.

After quickly learning how to care for a Cobra Gunship, I decided I wanted to fly. The Cobra Gunship flies with two pilots sitting in tandem, one behind the other. The rear pilot flies the gunship. The front pilot fires the weapon systems. Both know how to fly the Cobra Gunship. I convinced my Platoon sergeant to transfer me over to the Slicks (troop carrying helicopter). The Slick had two pilots sitting beside each other, a door gunner on the right rear door with an M-60 machine gun as a door gun and the left side was manned by the Crew Chief who also had a M-60 machine gun as a door gun. I flew on the left side. I was only a Slick Crew Chief for two weeks when I was medivaced to Okinawa for two and a half months. When I was sent back to Vietnam, I was assigned to the 1/10 Air Cav, D Troop who were using An Khe as their base camp. An Khe was occupied by the 4th Infantry Division. The concertina wire perimeter around the space the 4th Division occupied was 26 miles. It was a very large base camp. When I arrived at D Troop company area, I was sent to the Orderly Room (Administrative and Company Commander office). The CO (Company Commander), a Captain, came out of his office, introduced himself, and asked us if we were new in country. The other guy (who turned out to be a friend I met during state side duty) said he was, but I said I had entered country in July. This was December. The CO asked me what I had been doing. I told him I was a Crew Chief/Gunner on a Slick. I was returning to Vietnam after spending two and a half months in the hospital in Okinawa. He said they had all kinds of Slick Crew Chiefs. They did not need anymore. He assigned me and my friend to the Scouts. I thought to myself, "Holy Crap! I sure as hell did not want to do that!" I had been asked to join the Scouts when I was at Phan Thiet. The Scouts got shot at day in and day out by the enemy! A lot of them got wounded! I told them I was not stupid. Now, here I was being told I had to be a Scout.

They had a shortage of Scouts. Scouts are small helicopters that go out in helicopter teams known as Hunter/Killer Teams. A Scout was a small helicopter called a LOACH (Light

Observation Aerial Combat Helicopter) with only the pilot and the Crew Chief/Gunner. The Hunter/Killer Teams consisted of two Scouts, two Cobra Gunships, and a Slick. The two scouts did everything the grunts (infantry) did on the ground, except it was done from tree top level. Scout helicopters (LOACH) were very vulnerable to enemy ground fire and B-40 rockets (rocket grenade launcher). It is very easy to shoot a helicopter out of the sky if the enemy shooting at you does not get greased (killed) first! If the Scouts started receiving fire, they would mark the area with smoke grenades and the Cobra Gunships would roll in to destroy the area. They saved my butt more than once. Sometimes we just barely got out of the way before they let loose with their fire power. However, it had to be that way to save lives, especially mine. If a Scout or a Cobra Gunship was shot down, the Slick would swoop down to extract the pilots and the Crew Chief/Gunner out before they could be captured by the enemy. The Scout was an OH-58 Bell Ranger helicopter called a LOACH (Light Observation Aerial Combat Helicopter). It was quick and very maneuverable. These LOACH pilots were very, very good pilots (to me the best). I will share some stories about them later.

VIETNAM - M-60 MACHINE GUN – MY WEAPON OF DEATH

I am going to share with you how good I became with an M-60 machine gun, which was the weapon used on a scout LOACH that puts out 200 round per minute. One had to be careful how long a burst of rounds could be shot at one time because the barrel would get so hot it would stop firing. The infantry carried extra barrels and special asbestos gloves to change the barrels during a long firefight. They also carried an asbestos bag to carry the barrels in. We Scouts carried 2000 rounds of M-60 machine gun ammo. One ammo can was filled with 2000 rounds.

When I arrived in Vietnam, I made a pledge to myself I was going to return home alive. Being a crew chief/gunner on a Scout LOACH (Light Observation Aerial Combat Helicopter), I felt I needed to be exceptionally good with the M-60 machine gun I used to save the life of my pilot, me, and my fellow platoon members flying in the Hunter/Killer Team. We were returning to our base camp after a mission late one afternoon. My pilot and I were having a chit chat asking each other questions getting to know one another. I was training him on the strategies and techniques we used as a Hunter/Killer Team. I had a lot of experience and had flown on many combat missions. The pilot asked me how good I was with that M-60 machine gun. I told him I thought I was pretty good. He says, "Let's see how good you really are." Out about 100 yards in front of our Scout LOACH was a heron flying across. The heron is a decent sized bird in Vietnam. The pilot says, "Okay, let's just see how good you really are. Shoot that heron." I raised my M-60, gave it a 5-round burst (brrrrrp), and down goes the heron. The pilot says, "Damn, you are good with that thing! I want to fly with you from now on."

This pilot was serving his second Vietnam War tour. His first tour he was a Medivac (Dust-off) helicopter pilot. Those guys were the best! They had to land their Dust-off Chopper in an LZ (Landing Zone) the size of a postage stamp to pick up the wounded and the dead while receiving enemy fire (called a hot landing zone)! To keep from getting shot down, they had to get in and out in a heartbeat! Damn, they were good!

One of my platoon members and I were always asked to demonstrate the M-60 machine gun at the firing range for all the new guys (FNG's) coming in country. They all needed to be familiar with all the small weapons used in Vietnam. My friend and I would set number 10 cans out about 100 feet, start firing, lift the cans off the ground, and take them down about 200 yards or so without them hitting the ground. We received a lot of cheers and wows each time we did it. I could break down my M-60 weapon and put it back together again in seconds. That weapon became a part of me.

Vietnam - M-60 Machine Gun

Heron in South Vietnam

VIETNAM EXPERIENCE OF BLOWING UP ONE OF OUR HELICOPTERS

I WANT TO tell the story of the day I had the thrill of blowing up one of our helicopters. As Scouts, we went out in Hunter/Killer Teams. Two scout Light Observation Aerial Combat Helicopters (LOACH), two Cobra gunship helicopters, and one Slick (troop carrying) helicopter. At the time all of this happened we were supporting a team of LRRP's (Long Range Reconnaissance Patrol). These were a patrol of eight to ten infantrymen whose sole responsibility was to spy on the enemy. They normally went out for two weeks at a time. They were to avoid any contact with the enemy. Of course, that was not always possible. Often the Scouts were scrambled out to get the LRRP's out of trouble. They would be attacked, get pinned down, and call for help to eliminate loss of life or getting wounded. We were in contact with the enemy NVA forty-one days in a row.

On this particular day my Scout team was scrambled out to extract the LRRP's because the earlier extraction team had their Slick shot down. We relieved the earlier extraction team, our Slick extracted the LRRP's out while the rest of us stayed behind to secure the crash site. A radio call was made to Battalion headquarters to see how the situation should be handled. They said blow up the helicopter. That shocked us because normally they sent out a Chinook (large double propeller helicopter called

"Sh*t Hook) to hook on to the wreckage, take the wreckage to the rear, repair the damaged helicopter, or part it out. When the order came out to blow the Slick up, the Crew Chief/Gunner in the other Scout LOACH immediately informed me that he got to blow it up because he had been in country longer than me. I agreed, but stipulated he only got two chances to get it done. If he did not get the job done, then it was my turn. He told me I would never get the chance.

Each Scout LOACH carried an M-79 grenade launcher. It broke down in half to place a grenade (shaped like a fat bullet) into the chamber like a single-shot shot gun does. He and his pilot came around to the wreckage, he fired a grenade from his grenade launcher, and it landed in the passenger compartment. Boom! Nothing happened! He and his pilot came around again. He fired a grenade into the passenger compartment again. Nothing. Now it was my turn. I was told I would never get it done. I was training a new pilot. I asked him to get me as close to the wrecked helicopter as possible. I wanted my grenade to puncture the skin of the wrecked helicopter so it would go into the fuel tank. I told my pilot when he heard the thump of the grenade firing from the grenade launcher to get the hell out of Dodge. I fired, he left in a heartbeat, the grenade went into the fuel tank. It looked like an atomic bomb had gone off! There was a huge mushroom cloud. The fuel tank of the wrecked helicopter must have been full. Vietnam heard a scream and yell for miles around as I expressed my thrill and joy! I was so proud of myself! I gained quite a reputation for that deed! I had scores of soldiers and pilots look me up to get a first-hand story of this little adventure. I was told I was just lucky! You and I know differently, don't we? I have omitted the names of the rest of my Scout team because I have not received permission to use their names. I would not want to publicly embarrass the other Scout Crew/Chief Gunner even though I razzed the crap out of him. Trust me! These guys were some awesome fighters and pilots who were fantastic individuals. I am proud to have served with them! They know who they are!

*Vietnam - Chinook (Sh*t Hook) Helicopter*

M-79 Grenade Launcher Called The "Thumper"

Slick Helicopter Like The One I Blew Up

AFTER VIETNAM WAR EXPERIENCES

I AM GOING to share with you some things when I returned to "The World" (home) flying on the "Freedom Bird" (airplane home). I never became addicted to any drugs (except one which I will explain later), while in Vietnam, but drug addiction was rampant. I think I am safe in saying at least 50 percent of the military personnel were strung out on heroin or opium. With those who smoked marijuana while in Vietnam, that makes 75 percent of the military personnel using an illegal drug. One could buy a large freezer bag full of marijuana for five bucks. One could buy a vial of 98% pure heroin the size of your thumb for five bucks. Some would shoot it up using a syringe and needle, some would snort it, and others would sleeve a little bit of tobacco out of a cigarette, pour in the heroin, shake it down, and smoke it. The last method was most popular in my unit. The company leadership could not catch anyone using heroin because it did not smell any different from smoking a cigarette. At first the military would catch guys using heroin or opium, bring them in for a disciplinary court (Article 15), and bust them in rank. It never helped one bit. So, they decided to do random urine tests. Those who tested positive were sent to rehab. That did some good but did not solve the problem. No urine tests were done for marijuana. There were hundreds of military personnel that had to go to rehab before they could be sent home. Rehab was a cold turkey, quitting program without any drug assistance. Guys I have talked to that had to go through rehab said it was a tough and very painful four weeks before they were released.

I truly believe all the drug problems in Vietnam including smoking marijuana (called Dew or Can sa in Vietnamese) has contributed immensely to the drug problems in the 60's, 70's, and today in this country. So many people, including senior citizens, smoke marijuana. Several states have made recreational use of marijuana legal and more states are set to make it legal!

Now, about my addiction. I became really Gung HO in Vietnam. That means I wanted to go into battle all the time. Why? I was addicted to adrenaline, the natural stimulant drug in our body. When adrenaline is high, the butt hole puckers up. We measured how much the adrenaline high was by pucker factor. When we would come in off a mission, it was not uncommon for someone to ask how high the pucker factor was. I loved that adrenaline high. I was addicted to it. There were many others addicted as much as I was. We had a Congressional Medal of Honor winner join the ARP's (Aero Rifle Patrol), which was the infantry part of our company. Whenever they were out humping in the bush and they started to receive enemy fire, if the action came from the front and he was at the rear, he would run as fast as he could to get to the action. He wanted that adrenaline high he experienced in the battle that awarded him the Congressional Medal of Honor. It damn near got him killed several times. The ARP's had to ship him out somewhere else where he would not kill himself.

When a soldier, for a length of time, thinks about killing the enemy 24/7 before being killed himself, it takes a while to get out of that thinking mode even after returning home. I was living in Columbus, Ohio at the time (almost a year after I got home). My roommate (who is a Vietnam War veteran) and I wanted to go see a live band playing at a night club near the Ohio State University campus. I had a date. My roommate did not. When we walked in paying the cover charge at the entrance, off to the right was a young, scrawny, blonde-haired dude backing this big guy up to the wall and calling him a narc (someone who rats on drug users and dealers). We ignored the situation, walked into the night club, and tried to find a table to sit at. We did not see one immediately. I told my roommate and date to find us a table and I would buy a pitcher (the big thick glass ones) of beer. It took me a while to get to the bar to order the beer because of the large crowd about eight people deep. When I got to the bar, waiting for my pitcher of beer, I noticed this scrawny, blonde-haired guy giving me the evil eye from the end of the bar. I thought that was very strange and ignored it. I took the beer and cups into the main room of the night club, found my roommate and date, but no table. They were all occupied. We stood in place listening and watching the band when I felt something on the back of my long wool overcoat I was wearing. I turned around, but the table behind me acted as if nothing happened. My roommate came over and yelled into my ear (music was extremely loud) that a guy at the table behind me threw a beer on me. Not wanting to start any trouble and because the music was loud, I figured he tried to get my attention and I did not hear him. We were standing in the way of them seeing the band. I told my roommate and date we needed to go somewhere where we were not blocking anyone from watching the band.

We went clear across the other side of the room and stood against the wall. I had just finished pouring the last bit of beer into each of our paper cups from the glass pitcher when the scrawny, blonde- haired kid and eight other guys jumped up into my face. The scrawny, blonde-headed kid said that I was a narc. He told me that around there, narcs die! Something snapped in my head. I immediately threw my beer in his face, grabbed his throat with my left hand, and slammed him around into the wall behind me. I was coming down onto his head and face with the heavy glass empty pitcher when my roommate screamed into my ear, "Randy!!! Don't!!!" It was just enough to pull me out of my mind set. In my mind that kid was dead. I did not spend a year and a half in Vietnam, worrying if I would ever come home again, to have some punk kid threaten my life. Because of my adrenaline high, I was choking the kid to death. One of his buddies finally pulled on my arm causing me to lose my grip. The scrawny, blonde-haired kid went limping off holding his throat. Then, I turned around to deal with the other eight guys. By that time my roommate had fired up and the eight guys decided they wanted no part of two Vietnam veterans. The manager of the club came over and asked us to leave. We bitched and complained because we did not start it. Because the blonde-haired punk and his eight buddies were regular customers, we had to leave. The prick manager would not even return our cover charge.

My roommate and I thought for sure we were going to get jumped outside. We walked back to back for six blocks to make sure we were not going to be surprised. Later, we caught people watching our apartment. It concerned my roommate and me so much we purchased switch blade knives and mace. We started taking karate lessons. A few months later my roommate was visiting a friend of his at the Columbus police station. While there one of the officers from the narcotics squad came by to tell him he looked just like one of their undercover officers. Then it clicked. The scrawny, blonde-haired punk at the night club really did think we were narcs. He confronted me first because I was considerably bigger than my roommate (who looked like the undercover officer). Everything went back to normal after a month or so. But every time I thought later about what happened I would think to myself, if I would have killed or seriously injured that scrawny, blond-haired punk, I would have gone to prison for life. That scared the crap out me. I shiver each time I think about it. From that time forth, I made a conscious effort never to let myself reach that zone ever again. It has been hard, but I have been successful.

I never regretted going to Vietnam. I realized it was important that we be there to preserve the freedoms that we enjoy. That is not the case with most guys that went to Vietnam. They did not think we should be there, they hated it, and had a bad attitude about it. Not me! America has a lot of catching up to do to make it right for all those faithful young men, who accepted being drafted or volunteered, who ponied up, and went to a war they did not understand. They are all my brothers. That is why I have so much respect for our military today. They all do it voluntarily and for the love of their country, the United States of America!

America totally abandoned Vietnam War veterans. We were treated as outcasts. Our service to our country, when asked to do so, meant nothing. We left for Vietnam expecting nothing and when we returned nothing is what we got! The Veterans Administration had no answers or any desire to help suffering Vietnam veterans. The politicians scorned us. We were left to survive on our own. The deep pain, agony, and sorrow caused a lot of depression, anger, hurt, sobbing, alcoholism, and a high amount of illegal drug use. Many were searching for a way to kill the pain! We were crying out to you, yet you abandoned us! Why, America? Why? Many Vietnam War veterans could not stand the pain any longer. They chose to take their own life. Many ended up on the street homeless because they could not cope with everyday life. My Vietnam War brothers and I left a blank check for you willing to pay with our lives, if necessary, and signed it to preserve our country's way of life. You sure as hell cashed a bunch of them. Why did you treat us so poorly? Why could you not see our pain? We were crying out to you! Can you still help us? Are you willing to make a concentrated effort to seek out Vietnam veterans after all these years and help them put their demons to sleep for good? Can you see where your love, compassion, and genuine concern can heal the soul of a willing warrior? I challenge you, America, to make the commitment of sitting down with the Vietnam War veteran in your family, in your neighborhood, in your community to hug them, tell them how much you love them, and officially welcome them home. Convince them to write down their war experiences for their family history. Thank them for their service that has given you your comforts in life. Tell them you are deeply sorry and ask for their forgiveness. Cry with them! Celebrate with them! Let them feel important and needed once again! Buy this book as a gift for them. I leave you with tear-soaked pages! Thank you!

MY VIETNAM EXPERIENCE WITH A TWELVE HOLE LATRINE (TOILET)

UNWINDING IN VIETNAM was done in different ways. Some soldiers drank beer, some drank whiskey, some smoked marijuana (called Dew), some did heroin or opium. The beer sent over to Vietnam was sent green (not finished brewing). Then it sat out on the docks in the hot sun for several days. This made the beer taste skunky. It was terrible beer no matter what brand it was. One night I needed to get rid of some stress. I decided to go to the make-shift enlisted man's club to drink cans of beer. I guess I got rid of a little more stress than I anticipated. I stumbled back to my hooch, went to bed, and fell asleep. Early the next morning I woke up sitting on the toilet in the latrine (12-hole outhouse). I woke up that morning when all the guys started coming in to do their morning business. For the likes of me I do not know how I got there. It was not some place one wanted to be in the middle of the night. At night rats the size of cats would go in and out of the toilet holes looking for food particles. I got off the toilet, pulled my pants up, and went back to bed sick as a dog because the beer was so rotten. I suffered a sore butt for two days. I had a red ring around my butt for two weeks from sitting on that blasted toilet for so long. I never drank beer in Vietnam again after that experience.

Another experience I witnessed was when I was still at Phan

Thiet before I was medivaced to Okinawa. We had two outhouses (the Army calls them latrines) behind our hooch. One was used by the troops and the other was reserved for the hooch maids (Vietnamese woman hired to do our cleaning, washing, and ironing for $5 per month) to use. Vietnamese squat for everything. They were always squatting. They also squat when going to the bathroom by standing over the top of the toilet hole. This makes the toilet very messy and smelly because they sometimes miss the hole. They did not keep their toilet clean. They were very primitive in going to the bathroom. Early in the morning one would see the villagers going to the bathroom out in the rice paddies to fertilize the fields. Naturally they were always squatting.

We started catching the hooch maids going to the bathroom in our latrine. That really angered us because it made the toilet hole messy for us when we wanted to go to the bathroom. We chewed the hooch maids out, but there was one hooch maid that would not listen.

One morning one of our guys caught this hooch maid using our latrine again. The guy took a CS grenade (tear gas), threw it in the latrine, slammed the door shut, and locked it from the outside. The hooch maid could not get out. After she gagged, coughed, cussed (cussing in Vietnamese is hilarious), and screamed until the guy let her out. She was furious. We got our butts chewed out because the hooch maid belonged to the First Sergeant, the highest ranked enlisted man in the company. It sure cured the hooch maids from going into our latrine.

Vietnam - Two Hole Latrine (outhouse)

Vietnam - Hooch Maid Ironing Clothes

VIETNAM – WOUNDED BUTTOCKS STORY

MANY OF YOU have already read the Distinguished Flying Cross citation I posted earlier where I was wounded. I wanted to expound on that experience just a little bit. As the citation says, we were on a mission, received enemy fire, and had to roll out to let the Cobra Gunships roll in with their superior fire power. We had received information from intelligence sources there was NVA (North Vietnamese Army) movement in this certain sector of jungle. I was flying Lead Scout LOACH (Light Observation Aerial Combat Helicopter) that day. Lead Scout LOACH was the LOACH that did all the snooping and looking from tree top level. The Alpha Scout LOACH was the Loach that circled around the Lead LOACH when it came to a hover. In the jungle when a helicopter is flying overhead at tree top level, there is nothing but echo. Unless one cannot visually see the helicopter, you do not know where it is at exactly. As Scouts, we took advantage of that as a strategy. When the Lead LOACH came to a hover, the Alpha LOACH would circle around the Lead LOACH about 100 to 150 feet away. This even created even more confusion on the ground because the echo noise changed drastically as the Alpha LOACH did its circling. This helped us from being shot down. When we were fired at by the enemy, they were shooting haphazardly hoping to hit us by luck.

Our Hunter/Killer Team was looking for NVA movement surveying a large area in quadrants so we would not repeat looking in the same area over and over. We did find some enemy bunkers and reported them. We fired a couple of grenades into the bunkers from a Thumper (M-79 Grenade Launcher) and left that quadrant. We started searching another quadrant when all hell broke loose. I spotted enemy movement, started firing my M-60 machine gun, popped smoke to let the Cobra Gunships know where we engaged the enemy, and got the hell out of Dodge! As we were quickly leaving, there was a loud explosion. I thought the Cobra Gunships were firing down rockets already. They were good at laying down fire quickly so we would not get shot down. The Cobra Pilots related later they saw an explosion right below us about tree top level. We figured the NVA shot a B-40 Rocket at us. Our pilots were so good getting us out of harm's way. It is a fun sight to see these pilots react in unison as if they are putting on an act for an air show. What is so amazing to me and weird is the Crew/Chief Gunner flying the Alpha Loach was in a position where he did not see anything. He just heard the explosion. Another amazing thing is no damage was done to either helicopter. Not even a scratch. My butt was the target. When we fired our M-60 machine gun out of the left, front door of the Scout LOACH, we usually put our left foot on the helicopter runner and leaned way out the door to expand our firing radius. Doing that exposed our left leg and butt cheek. The pucker factor was off the chart on that one, but I loved every minute of it. I was addicted to adrenaline! I got a hell of a fix of it that day!

As we were returning to base camp at An Khe, I happened to look down at the runner (the skids the helicopter lands on) of my Scout LOACH to notice some blood. I was wondering where in the world that came from. I felt no pain. Adrenaline kills pain. I rubbed my butt/thigh only to have blood on my hand. I still really did not know where the blood was coming from. I told my pilot, whose call sign was Shamrock 17 (similar to a CB handle name, except Shamrock and a number were used for our pilots), I thought I was hit. He asked me where. I told him I did not know for sure but there was blood on the skid.

His eyes got big, he radioed the team leader I was wounded, he notified base camp we were coming in, and he kicked that helicopter into high gear. In fact, he had that helicopter going at such a high speed, it was vibrating and shaking. I kept telling him my wound did not feel very serious. He could slow down so the helicopter would not shake to pieces. That is the fastest I ever flew in a Scout LOACH in all the times I flew in one. Shamrock 17 (the pilot) landed in front of the Medical Aid Station, where the medical personnel were. I jumped out of the chopper and immediately dropped my pants shooting all of Vietnam a moon (we did not wear underwear because the heat caused severe rashes) trying to see where I was hit. Shamrock 17 told me later he wished he had not witnessed that. Every time he thinks about this incident, my moon comes to his mind. The medics came out immediately, grabbed me, took me to a metal table, laid me out, and started looking. The doctor saw it immediately. A piece of shrapnel had lodged in my body. The doctor took a medical tool, stuck it in the wound trying to pull out the piece of shrapnel, but gave up because it was too deep. The doctor said he would do more damage than good if he kept trying. He said he was not worried about infection, because the shrapnel went into my body so hot that it cauterized the wound. I was medivaced to an in-country hospital at Qui Nhon. I was there for two weeks just to make sure my wound did not become infected. I came home with a piece of shrapnel in me, but somewhere over time the last few years, the shrapnel worked its way out of my body. It is no longer there as a result of the VA medical personnel doing an ex-ray to see if it was still there. VA really takes excellent care of me. I am a 40-percent disabled Veteran. They have replaced both of my hips and both of my knees due to old age and arthritis. They bring me in every six months for a checkup. They provide any medication I need. They also bring me in to trim my toe nails every three months. The bottom of my feet have no feeling. Every time I trim my own toe nails, I cut them too short and they bleed. My VA doctor saw that, chewed me out, and said no more of that. Can't beat that, huh? Here in Ohio VA medical care is top notch. I have no complaints whatsoever. They have exceeded my expectations time after time. The only complaint I have is their hospital food is disastrous. It is one of those force-it-down or go hungry type of things. I was promised they were working on their food quality. It reminds me a lot of the food I had while still on active duty in the Army.

Vietnam - Scout LOACH after 1969

Vietnam - Calvary Hat Worn By Helicopter Pilots

Vietnam - Scout LOACH Crew Chief/Gunner And Pilot

VIETNAM – THE ZIPPO CIGARETTE LIGHTER

WHILE IN COLLEGE I started smoking a pipe because I thought it was cool. Because there were only ten minutes between classes, smoking a pipe was inconvenient. So, I switched to cigarettes. Besides the cigarettes, the most important thing I carried was my Zippo lighter. I smoked cigarettes in Vietnam then stopped when I had about six months of time left before I came home. The Zippo lighter became a way for soldiers to display their feelings by having sayings or short messages inscribed on them. These inscribed Zippo cigarette lighters became extremely popular with the troops. Those of you who are familiar with the Zippo lighter or still use one, it is a very reliable lighter. The only thing I did not like about it was when it was freshly filled with lighter fluid and stuck it in my pocket. Some of the fluid would escape, soak through to the leg, and cause a stinging feeling. This was very uncomfortable. I could not wait for my Zippo lighter to be used enough where the stinging would go away. I think you will find some of the messages on the pictured Zippo cigarette lighters from the Vietnam War are very interesting. It lets us all in on the attitude of the Vietnam War soldiers.

Vietnam - My Zippo Cigarette Lighter

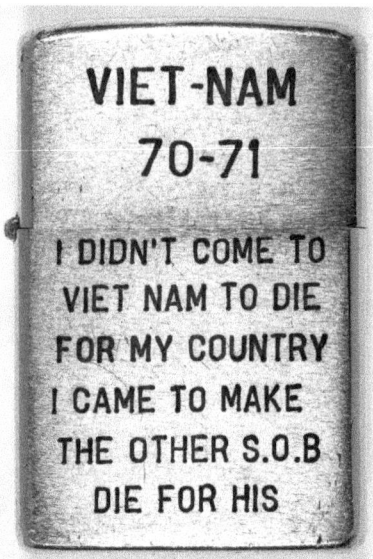

Vietnam - A Friend's Zippo Lighter

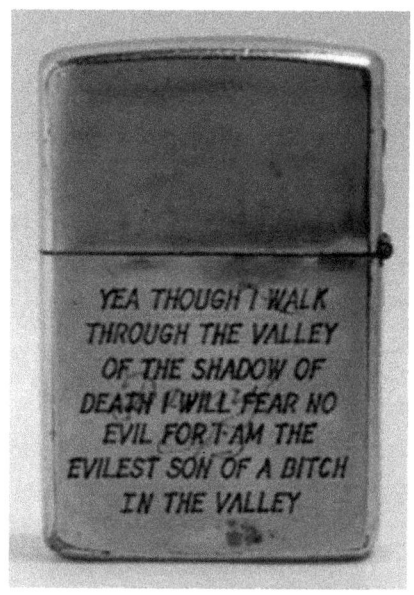

VIETNAM – DISCOVERING ONE OF MY UNIQUE ABILITIES

FOR SOME REASON I was blessed with the unique ability to understand the mechanics of a helicopter. I was a Crew Chief for a Cobra Gunship my first two months in Vietnam. Then, I became a Crew Chief/Gunner on a Slick (troop carrying helicopter) until I was medivaced to Okinawa for two and a half months. When I returned, I became a Crew Chief/Gunner on a Scout LOACH (Light Observation Aerial Combat Helicopter) for the rest of my tour. Being raised on a ranch and farm, I had learned to turn a wrench on tractors and machinery. I also did repairs on my own car. My senior year of high school I drove a 1946 Ford with a standard transmission. Twice that year I had to do my own repair on the transmission. Third gear had gone out twice. However, I never really considered myself a mechanic. But, because I understood the workings of a helicopter, the pilots liked to fly my helicopter because they knew I knew. The supervisor of the maintenance hangar would come get me when the maintenance crew could not figure out what was wrong with a helicopter. I would ask what had been done, study the problem, then suggest a fix. Sure enough, I was usually right! Why, I do not know! As I said, it was one of my unique abilities. The maintenance supervisor kept trying to get me transferred to maintenance. There was no way I was going to give up flying. It was too much fun and I was addicted to adrenaline. The upper brass even sent me to an engine school in the rear (out of the battle field) at Bien Hoa for two weeks to learn how to repair engines. I never understood that move. When an engine went bad, we sent the engines to the rear for maintenance. Our maintenance crew did not have the time nor the equipment to work on helicopter engines. One of the neat things though, is I ran into my best Army buddy who was serving in Bien Hoa. We were able to spend some time together and catch up. We later became roommates when I moved to Columbus, Ohio (his home town) after we returned from Vietnam and were discharged.

Vietnam - Inside the Scout LOACH Maintenance Hanger

*Repairing Two Scout LOACH's
Outside The Maintenance Hanger*

MY EXPERIENCES ON R&R FROM VIETNAM IN THAILAND

I WAS ENTITLED to four R&R's (rest and recuperation) because of the time I spent in Vietnam. I took only three. I went to Taipei, Taiwan (Nationalist China) twice and Bangkok, Thailand once. We were entitled to one week off. I want to share my experiences in Bangkok, Thailand. When I arrived in Bangkok, I did not have any civilian clothes. So, I bought a couple pair of nice pants and shirts along with some shoes. I hired a tour guide who wanted to take me up river to an island that had a zoo and a show arena. I put on a pair of new pants and a new shirt, as well as my new shoes.

We took about an hour ride up river to this island. It was pretty, but quite a few people were wandering around doing tourist things. We went to the zoo first. While wandering through the zoo looking at all the interesting animals, I decided I was thirsty. I bought a quart of Thai beer. It was really quite good tasting beer, especially after the pukey beer I drank in Vietnam. I kept walking around the zoo, cage to cage, only to come upon the cage with this huge Himalayan Grizzly Bear. It was absolutely huge. It looked just like the American Grizzly Bear except it had unquestionably long hair. I was standing, leaning on the iron bar that supposedly kept people a safe distance from the bear, sipping on my beer, and watching this monstrous animal. He suddenly gets up on his hind legs, walks over to the bars of the cage, sticks his arms and paws through the bars, and acts like he is asking for a drink of my beer. I had drank about one quarter of it. I thought, what the heck, let him have a beer. I handed my beer to the bear and he proceeded to jug my beer. I was trying like crazy to get it back from him, but he finished the beer and threw the bottle on the ground. I thought my tour guide was going to die of a heart attack from laughing. There was all kind of chatter because the tourists were taking pictures of this spectacle. Hell, now I have my picture scattered all over the world showing that bear stealing my beer.

We left the zoo to go to the show arena. They put on demonstrations of kick boxing, Thai dancing, and other acts that were interesting. One of the Thai dances is where they take long boards, bang them on the ground, and then bang them together. The dancers stepped in and out of the boards before their ankles were crushed. I was impressed with the athleticism of the dancers to be able to do that. After the demonstration was over, the dancers decided they needed someone from the crowd to do the dance for them. I tried to hide, but to no avail. They dragged my butt out, started the music, started banging the boards, and told me to dance in and out of the boards. I guess it was a good thing that bear drank my beer. I thought for sure I would end up in the hospital with broken ankles. My tour guide didn't make me feel any better either when I was told that was the funniest dance ever.

Next out came the guy from India with the basket and a cobra in it. He was a snake charmer. He set the basket down, took the lid off, and proceeded to play his flute. Nothing. He would reach into the basket and slap the crap out that cobra. I thought, holy crap, that sucker is going to mess around and get bit by the most poisonous snake in the world. The snake charmer reached into the basket three more times before the snake finally came out, spread out his hooded neck, and swayed back and forth to the music of the flute. After the show was over, the snake charmer was standing outside the arena with his snake and basket sitting on the ground. I went over to him to ask if his snake was defanged. He said most certainly. He would never reach into the basket and slap the snake otherwise. I told him I had never held a cobra before and asked if I could hold it. He said "Sure!" He reached down into the basket, grabbed the snake, and laid it in my outstretched hands. Wow, that was weird! I was holding a live cobra! Well, the cobra decided he did not like it. It started to wiggle and jump all over. My natural reflex was to squeeze tight to hold onto the snake. That damn snake crapped up and down my new pants, because I squeezed too hard. The snake charmer and my tour guide thought that was the funniest thing they had ever seen. My tour guide wanted to be hired by me the next day, because laughing at me was so fun.

MY VIETNAM RAT EXPERIENCE

IN 1971 THE U.S. government started sending troops home. The Marines had all been sent home already. Now it was time to send the 4th Division home which is the Division my Battalion and Company were part of. The 4th Division resided in the base camp of An Khe. It was so large, the border of the camp was 26 miles in perimeter. That is bigger than my home town I live in now, Zanesville, Ohio, which has approximately 28,000 people. An Khe did not have that much population, but the land area was bigger.

I was assigned to the detail of soldiers left behind to guard all the buildings of a certain area until everything was moved out and abandoned. There were six of us guarding my assigned area. We took turns in shifts. My bunk was in the corner of the hooch to the right of the front door. One night one of our ARP's (Aero Rifle Patrol infantryman) was sitting in the doorway sharpening his machete used to cut and remove brush when they were humping out in the jungle. I could never sleep very well while in Vietnam. If a person walked up to my bunk, they would be immediately staring at a .38 caliber pistol in my right hand and my left hand on my M-16 automatic rifle. I was sensitive because I always feared enemy Sappers (kind of like our special forces only more primitive) would invade our perimeter wire, throw satchel charges into our hooch, and blow the hell out of everything.

I heard this whoosh, whoosh from the ARP swinging his machete, the footsteps of something pitter pattering on the floor, felt it jump up on my bunk, run up my body (I was laying on my left side), hit the head of my bunk, turn right on my face, and head down the wall and floor the other direction. Then I heard another whoosh, whoosh down the wall a short distance, another pitter pattering, the thing landed on my face, turned to go down my body, and I felt the whoosh, whoosh over my body. That is when I jumped up, grabbed the ARP, and asked him what the crap he was doing. He said he was trying to kill a rat as big as a cat with a tail the size of one's thumb. I said, not over my body you are not. I may have needed a haircut and a shave, but not that badly. That is why I would not eat a hamburger in Vietnam that was not served in our mess hall. The Vietnamese used rats and dogs to make their hamburgers. It definitely was not like eating at McDonald's!

We had to live in tents for a short period of time after our company left An Khe until another unit moved out of our permanent quarters. The tents were hot and smelled with a mildew smell. It took a bit to get used to.

Vietnam - What We Called "Tent City"

VIETNAM FRAGMENT GRENADE STORY

ON DAYS THAT I was not flying on missions as a Crew Chief/Gunner on a Scout LOACH (Light Observation Aerial Combat Helicopter) as a Scout in a Hunter/Killer Team, I would be lying around my hooch (living quarters) catching up on sleep or reading a paperback book. Occasionally, our First Sergeant would ask us to do things for him. One day he asked us to build a protection bunker for outside the company headquarters so when there was incoming enemy mortar rounds, the company leadership would have somewhere safe to go. We commandeered a deuce and a half truck, grabbed a bunch of empty sandbags, headed for the nearest beach (about 20 miles away), and proceeded to fill several hundred sandbags. I do not want to tell a lie! It was extremely hot out; way too hot to work hard filling sandbags. We hired Papa-son (older Vietnamese civilian man) and his son to fill them for us. They were used to the heat and they were very hard workers. We spent the few hours it took them to fill the sandbags in the shade. When the deuce and a half was full of sandbags, we paid Papa-son the twenty dollars we owed him, went back to our base camp, unloaded the sandbags while building the bunker, and went to lunch. The First Sergeant could not believe we built that bunker in half a day. Whenever he asked other platoons to do this, it took them two days to build a bunker. That is why we did not have to get up early each morning for company formation (where the whole company lined up for roll call and to receive instructions for the day). We had permission to sleep in. We earned this privilege with hard work and team work.

Our company commander, a Captain, went on R&R (Rest and Recuperation) for a week. Our platoon leader, a Captain (we called him Dai uy -pronounced Da Wee - which means Captain in Vietnamese) was appointed temporary company commander. Dai uy had not been in our company long enough to lose all his state side officer attitude of "do what I say" in the wrong way for a war zone. We had not had enough time to work that attitude out of him yet. In our company we did not salute officers or call them "Sir." We called them by first name or nicknames. My time in Vietnam was like a regular state side job. One respects the authority of those in charge, but the conversations were usually not military etiquette. Dai uy decided to start coming down on the "Heads" (drug users) and harass them. He pissed them off. In Vietnam if an officer got out of line and angered his men, he was fragged. In-other-words, he was killed or injured very seriously with a fragment grenade. The "Heads" knew that would not solve their problem. They were smarter than that. It would only bring more heat down on them. Our regular company commander let them hide under the trouble radar as long as they behaved themselves and did their jobs without incident.

Our hooch's were built on concrete slabs. They were six-inch lap siding a third of the way up. The rest of the wall was screening for ventilation. The roof was corrugated metal sheets. Sandbags were stacked around the hooch the same height as the lap siding. This gave us protection from in-coming mortars when we hit the floor.

I was lying on my bunk (I had the top bunk just high enough to be above the sandbags) reading a book when a soldier from another platoon from the hooch next door hollered at me and said, "Randy, come here right away!" The urgency in his voice caused me to jump out of my bunk, hit the floor, and run out to where the soldier was. He was standing outside my hooch right where my bunk was. He had been sitting on the sandbags smoking a cigarette. He pointed out a fragment grenade down in the sandbags with the pin pulled and a rubber band wrapped around it to keep it from exploding. It would do some serious damage, especially to me and maybe the guy who slept below me. With the heat, humidity, and the wet atmospheric conditions in Vietnam, it did not take long for a rubber band to rot. Maybe two or three days, perhaps. The pin was lying by the grenade. I exploded! I was pissed! I knew exactly who had put the grenade there, why, and they knew how I would react. You see? I made a pact to myself, when I first entered Vietnam. I was coming home alive and in one piece, bar none!

I grabbed the grenade with the rubber band still on it and the loose pin. I marched over to the company headquarters, stormed into the commanding officer's office, and threw the pin of the grenade on the desk in front of Dai uy! Then, I laid the rubber band laden grenade along beside the pin. Dai uy's eyes got huge and he backed up away from the desk. He thought I had come to frag him. I told him to calm down, I was not going to frag him, but I was thoroughly pissed. I told him where I found the grenade, who put it there (the "Heads"), and he had better back off the "Heads" or I would frag him. Well, my point was well taken. I put the pin back in the grenade so Dai uy could breathe normal again. Dai uy apologized to me and he did back off harassing the "Heads." Dai uy and I had a lot of respect for each other. He knew I was good at my job. He flew as my pilot many times. He also knew about my pact to myself that I was going home alive and in one piece.

In war, attitudes change, sometimes for the good, and sometimes for the bad, but mostly for the bad! Depression and anger do not mix well! Fear of the unknown drives individuals nuts in war. That fear drives up the depression and anger. Then, to add lack of sleep and lack of the comforts of life to that, it can get mighty lonely! I love my fellow Vietnam veterans. These guys had to go through stuff that others do not even come close to understanding. I have a Vietnam veteran acquaintance who had to retire at the age of 53. His wife had left him. His children wanted to stay away from him. He could not keep a job. He was finally diagnosed by VA with PTSD (Post Traumatic Stress Disorder) thirty-three years after returning home from Vietnam. He is now receiving the medical care and the disability pay he deserves. It just came thirty-three years too late for him to have the enjoyable life he is entitled to. I cry every time I think about it.

His time in the Vietnam War was miserable for him. He came to Vietnam as an 18-year-old kid. He served his whole time as a grunt (infantry) wallowing around in the mud, enduring the intense heat and humidity, tolerating the putrid smell of the jungle, and shaking with fear never knowing if he would be coming back home! Later in this book I have statistics about the names on the Vietnam War Memorial Wall in Washington, DC. You will be shocked!

This is the plight of many Vietnam Veterans. Many have weathered the storm, but the storm damage is still there. They have just covered it up. Their families know, though, especially wives. They see pain and they see suffering in simple ways. I thank God for those who are helping my Vietnam brothers heal. I hope I can do my part!

Vietnam - What Our Hooch (Living Quarters) Looked Like

Vietnam - Fragment Grenade

VIETNAM – TRAINING TO SURVIVE

THE VIETNAM WAR preparation started in basic training in the Army! In basic training in 1969, we originally started training with the M-14 Rifle, which is a bolt action rifle. They were reasonably heavy, but we got in shape as we marched or double timed (running) with them repeating stupid chants. I shot expert with the M-14. It is a rifle with a very accurate, peep hole rear site with an open site on the barrel! Targets would pop up as far as 300 yards (three times the length of a football field) shooting to knock them down! We switched over to the M-16 Automatic Rifle two-thirds of the way through basic training. I was stationed at Ft. Lewis, Washington. We practiced with the M-16 at the firing range getting more effective with knocking down the pop-up targets. I shot expert with the M-16 Automatic Rifle also. In addition to that I received expert in grenade throwing, received a perfect score in the physical training test, received a 100 percent score in the G-3 test. This test included drill and ceremony, hand to hand combat, bayonet combat, and a written test. I also was the company champion in pugil stick fighting (used to beat the crap out of each other simulating hand-to-hand combat with a rifle). The pugil stick is a plastic stick with Styrofoam type padding on each end.

The physical training test consisted of running a mile under a certain time in combat boots, a timed race on the monkey bars, a timed run, dodge, and jump course, a timed dead-man-carry race carrying someone your own weight a certain distance, and a timed low crawl race crawling under low bars close to the ground! That all came about because our drill sergeant had us out training constantly instead of cleaning and shining our barracks. We were the recipients of the eight-ball award every day I was in basic training. Our drill sergeant called us the "the Outcast-es." He assigned me as a squad leader because I had run my own logging crews in the logging camps of Alaska!

We were told 35 percent of the graduating trainees would be advanced from E-1 Private to E-2 Private. That meant a raise from $88 per month to $101 per month. I really wanted the money! Even at $101 per month a soldier would be broke in the middle of the month! Imagine getting only $88 per month! Working so hard to get that extra money and stripe ended up getting me awarded the "Outstanding Trainee of the Cycle" that resulted in me receiving five trophies and a ten-minute hand shake from the Battalion Colonel at graduation time.

I can thank my high school football coach for teaching me to work hard at physical things since he loved to torture us with wind sprints at the end of every football practice. This was after we worked our tails off in practice, tired tails! Then we had to run the half mile or so from the baseball field, where we practiced on the outskirts of town, to the dressing room at the high school. I will say, he had us in good shape. Coach was like a drill sergeant! That was the kind of shape I was in at the end of basic training.

When I arrived in Vietnam, I was issued my M-16 Automatic Rifle. After arrival at my permanent duty station, Phan Thiet on the coast of the South China Sea, I had to pull guard duty on the perimeter of the base camp. The guard towers I was always assigned to by the Sergeant of the Guard were the towers overlooking the beach. Maybe he knew I shot expert with an M-16. At night the Vietnamese fishermen would come out in their fishing boats using lanterns to light their way. I had it in my mind that it would be very easy for a fisherman to ease up close to the beach to drop off some Sappers (enemy Special Forces) who would then sneak through our perimeter wire and wreak holy havoc. We fired off flares that would light up the sky to see if anyone was trying to breach our perimeter. Many a night the fishermen with their lighted fishing boats would inch closer to the beach. I kept thinking about how a python will kill their prey. They inch closer and closer, scaring the prey each time the snake moves; the python would let the prey settle down then move again until the snake had the prey wrapped into a death squeeze. I thought I had to let the fishermen know I was on to them. No python moves on our base camp! Each of our M-16 clips held thirty rounds with every fourth round being a red tracer round for night detection. This let me know if I was hitting what I was firing at in the night. I regularly lit up a Vietnamese fishing boat because I felt they were getting too close. My fellow soldiers on guard duty could not believe how accurate I was at hitting those boats, especially the ones that were farther out. That is a result of that firing range training in basic training.

Triple canopy jungle presented a lot of problems for the U.S. Military. With its three layers of foliage, thickness, and darkness inside, it was not a pleasant place to go into. On one of our missions our Hunter/Killer Team came across six enemy elephants. One could tell they were enemy elephants because they had strap marks on them from having backpacks strapped to them. Knowing these elephants were used to resupply ammunition, supplies, and troops to the enemy, something had to be done with them. The Mission Leader (usually one of the Cobra pilots) called the situation into the Battalion Headquarters. The Battalion Commander ordered the team to herd them into the base camp. Everyone looked at their pilots, muttered disbelief over the radio between helicopters, and were shocked at such a request. How in the world do you herd six elephants from a helicopter? However, an order is an order. Our team started to herd the elephants along. It was going along a lot better than anticipated until they went into triple canopy jungle. The jungle was so thick those six elephants could not be seen from the air. The mission leader called back into Battalion Headquarters that the elephants were lost. The Battalion Commander, an egotistical Colonel, came on the radio and said, "How in the hell do you lose six elephants?" Well, our team lost them! As the team was leaving, one elephant decided to come back out. I am not going to tell you what the outcome was for that elephant because I do not want animal rights activists picketing anyone's house. All I am going to say is one of the Scout LOACH (Light Observation Aerial Combat Helicopter) Crew Chief/Gunners came back to base camp with 2000 (whole ammo can full) fewer M-60 Machine gun rounds of ammunition and the elephant was dead!

Both Scout LOACH's carried an M-79 grenade launcher on board! We used it to blow up enemy bunkers and fire concussion grenades into tunnel openings when we found them! The concussion grenades would blow out the enemy's ear drums causing them to bleed to death! Hey! This is war! The toughest soldier wins!

One of our LOACH pilots was leaving to go home in three days! He had always wanted to fly on a mission as a Scout LOACH gunner! We decided we would give him the opportunity. That was a bad mistake! He did not pay attention enough as we were firing our weapons. They came across a bunker he wanted to blow up. He loaded the M-79 grenade launcher, cocked it, brought it up to his shoulder, and fired. He laid his head on the butt of the launcher making his head too close to the latch on the rear that one pushes to the side to open the launcher; like one opens a double -barreled shot gun to load it. When the pilot (thinking he was a gunner) fired the launcher, the launcher reared back shoving the latch into his eye causing him to lose his eye. It made his stay in Vietnam a few days longer. When he came by after being let out of the hospital to say his goodbyes, he told all of us he would keep an eye out for us!

Many times, as we were searching the jungle from tree top level looking for the enemy, we would come across tribes of mountain people, who hated the North Vietnamese and Viet Cong, but loved us. They were the Montagnards (pronounced mountain yards). They were very tribal. We always knew which women were married and which women were not married. The married women went topless! We thought that was a very strange custom! They were always smiling and waving at us. They were good people to have on our side.

South Vietnam had been at war for so many years, their citizens did not even have the slightest idea what they were fighting for. Most of them were fighting for survival. The ones who became our friends were sad to see our soldiers leave for good. Their standard of living improved immensely from our being there. That is why so many refugees left South Vietnam to come to the United States, the land of opportunity and freedom. Go USA!

Vietnam - Guard Tower

Vietnam - M-16 Automatic Rifle

*M-79 Grenade Launcher Showing
The Latch That Took Pilot's Eye Out*

VIETNAM – A LITTLE, ORNERY, WILD SIDE

AS I PONDER about those I served with, the relationships we had and how we worked so hard to cover each other's butts, I am so grateful for associating with so many quality individuals. I never ran into an American soldier I did not like! We also had a little wild side! Sometimes while on a mission, we would come across marijuana drying racks. The marijuana growing in Vietnam was very tall and it was plentiful. The North Vietnamese Army (NVA) would grow it, harvest it, and lay it out on drying racks exposing it to the hot sun. When the marijuana was marketable, they would sell it to the American soldiers. A soldier could by a large freezer bag full (called a bushel) for $5. Marijuana was called Dew or Can Sa (Vietnamese).

As you look around your own community and sphere of influence to see how many individuals smoke marijuana, a person can visualize how many soldiers smoked marijuana. The NVA (North Vietnamese Army) made a lot of money to fund their war efforts by selling marijuana to our side. Because these drying racks of marijuana belonged to the enemy, we had to burn them to hurt them financially. We would hover over the racks, drop incendiary grenades (grenades that started fires), and let them burn. Naturally, we had to hang around for a minute or two to make sure they were burning properly! Flying back and forth over the fire, breathing in the smoke, making sure we were destroying the NVA money pit, made some exceptionally happy helicopter fly boys by the time we got back to base camp. Come on! You did not expect us to hold our breath while checking out these burning racks of marijuana, did you?

Another grenade we carried was a smoke grenade! We carried several colors! The purpose of the smoke grenades was for marking locations. While out in our Hunter/Killer Teams, if the Scout LOACH's started receiving enemy fire, we would holler over the radio "Receiving fire! Receiving fire!" We would pop smoke. The Cobra Gunships became aware of the vicinity where we engaged the enemy. Each time the "Grunts" (infantry men) were being extracted (taken out of the jungle), they would pop smoke to let the "Slick" (troop carrying helicopter) know where the "LZ" (landing zone) was. When the Medivac Helicopters ("Dust Off" Helicopter) came in, smoke grenades marked where they were to land to pick up the wounded and dead. I have the highest respect for "Dust Off" pilots. They had to be so skilled. They could land their helicopter on what looked like a postage stamp sized area in the jungle and not hit any trees with their rotors.

We used the red smoke grenade whenever we returned from a mission after getting a kill (killed an enemy soldier). Our Scout LOACH's would low-level (fly 3 to 4 foot off the ground) along the runway of our air strip with the Crew Chief/Gunner holding a red smoke grenade with smoke trailing behind to let the whole base camp know we got a kill. This seemed to be a morale booster. There was a lot of hate for the enemy who was killing some of our friends. Lots of questions were asked by many about the mission.

Making the trip back in from missions sometimes would present some interesting happenings. When the weather was nice, the Vietnamese, unmarried girls from the villages of the "Friendlies" (Vietnamese on our side) would be down at the river near their village bathing. We would come along low-level-flying (3 to 4 feet off the water) scaring the crap out of these young women. We were able to get some great nude looks. They would rush out of the water shaking their fists back at us. That was the pornography experiences we had in Vietnam! Naked girls!

Another flying assignment we had was a bit boring. It was guarding truck convoys coming through An Khe Pass. When the French were fighting in South Vietnam, they were attacked, passing through the An Khe Pass, when the enemy launched an attack killing or wounding approximately 10,000 French soldiers. The upper brass did not want that to happen to our convoys. Some of these truck convoys were very long carrying important cargo to re-supply many of the base camps. Believe it or not the highway was paved. Most of the convoys would have a flatbed semi-truck that would be empty because it was unloaded at an earlier base camp. It never failed we would have to have a little fun with these guys. My Scout LOACH pilot would show off low-level-flying, which got a lot of cheers from the truck drivers. What I liked the most is when he would land our helicopter on the back of one of the empty flatbeds. That takes a lot of flying skill to land a flying helicopter on a moving flatbed truck! The reaction from the truck driver was priceless. He would see the shadow of our helicopter thinking we were flying over him only to realize we were not moving past him. We would invariably get the old double look with shock, surprise, and then howling laughter. I always got a belly laugh over that one! We got a lot of air horns honking expressing their approval. As I mentioned earlier, we had a little bit of wild side to us and it was fun!!

Vietnam - Scout LOACH Low Leveling Over A River

Vietnam - Covering A Convoy From The Air

Vietnam - Scout LOACH Low Leveling After A KIll

VIETNAM – MY EXPERIENCES WITH RACIAL TENSION

I had never experienced racial tensions before. Being raised on a 3000-acre ranch outside of Timber Lake, South Dakota, it was not something we had to deal with. Some of our neighbors were Native Americans who were great neighbors. I went to high school with a Native American who ended up losing his life in Vietnam. He was a football star. One of my roommates in college was Native American. Racial tension was not in the equation. I did not have any experiences with African Americans until I was drafted into the Army.

My first experience with an African American was in basic training. He was in my platoon. I did not get to know him well because he slept on the second floor of our barracks and was in a different squad than I was. I did know his name and where he was from. This guy was tall, extremely muscular with huge arms, thighs like tree trunks, a huge chest, a six-pack stomach, and a little waist. He was a dedicated weight lifter before being drafted. Everyone liked him. He was a very nice young man.

My drill sergeant was black also. He was from Georgia. His goal was to train us to be prepared to fight in Vietnam and survive. While the other platoons were spending time spit shining their barracks and kissing the Company Commander's buttocks, our platoon was out training and getting in physical shape. Every day when we returned to our barracks, before eating our evening meal, we saw the eight-ball award hanging over the front door of the barracks. Our drill sergeant would laugh! He called us the "Outcast-es" in his Georgia accent! We loved him and respected him. We gave him a special pocket watch upon basic training graduation that said, "From the Outcast-es!" It brought tears to his eyes. He knew we loved him.

One portion of our training was hand-to-hand combat. "Pugil stick" battles were designed to teach us to do hand-to-hand battle with our rifles. The pugil stick was approximately four feet long with Styrofoam type padding on each end. We would pair off, attack our opponent, and try to knock him on his butt. It was very hard not to get knocked on one's butt! After one week of pugil stick fighting, the company leadership wanted to have a pugil stick championship. We were divided into brackets, paired off with our assigned opponent, worked our way up the bracket (if we won our bracket), then waited for the championship battle. I happened to make it to the championship. The huge black kid in my platoon made it also. I looked at him and thought, "I am going to get killed! I am going to experience a lot of pain!" When our battle was announced, I quickly was trying to think of a strategy to keep me from getting destroyed. As the pugil stick was handed to me and we were asked to start the battle, a strategy came into my mind. Before, in practice training and during the contest, opponents would charge each other running, screaming, and yelling trying to intimidate their opponent. I decided I would approach the giant by walking towards him cautiously locking his eyes on my eyes. When I approached him with his eyes locked on mine, I struck quickly like a snake, slamming him in the gut with lightning bolt speed bending him over. Then I hit him on the chin with a power stroke using my pugil stick to knock him flat on his back. I immediately proceeded to beat his face and head while standing over him. I was not going to let this monster of a man get up and knock me out (knock me out is what he would have done). Four drill sergeants rushed in to pull me off my opponent. As I walked past my drill sergeant, I threw my pugil stick to him and said, "I was not going to let Goliath win!" I received an award for that win at graduation time. None of the mouthy punks or bullies ever got smart with me after that! I earned their respect.

The next experiences I had with African Americans was in Vietnam. When I arrived at my permanent duty station in Phan Thiet, South Vietnam, I noticed the black guys raising their arms, forming a fist, shaking their fist (fist flopping back and forth at the wrist very quickly) as they passed each other. When they would stand to talk face to face, they would fist bump, elbow bump, shoulder bump, hip bump, and head bump. I kept asking why are they doing that? I was told it showed black solidarity and that black was beautiful. None of this bothered me, but the white guys from the south and big cities did not like it. As far as I was concerned there is a lot of black beauty out there. Let them claim it!

It did cause some racial tension, though! While stationed at An Khe, we had to go on a mission several miles away. After our mission, it was getting too late to make it back to our base camp before dark. Helicopters had to fly with their lights on at night to keep from hitting each other. The lights made us sitting ducks for the enemy. The officer in charge of our mission decided we would stay overnight in Ban Me Thuot (ban me too it).

After eating our evening meal, three of my fellow Scouts and I decided to walk around to see if anything exciting was going on. We heard music, walked towards the music, and found the Enlisted Men's Club had a live Vietnamese band with go-go girls. We walked into the entrance door, walked out onto a platform that had stairs going down to the main floor, and looked for a place to sit. The place was packed. One third of the crowd were black soldiers; the rest were white soldiers. Since we could not find a place to sit, my three Scout buddies and I decided to stand on the platform, listen to the band, and watch the go-go girls. This went on for about a half hour when in an instant all hell broke loose! Black guys were hitting white guys over the head with chairs and white guys were hitting black guys over the head with chairs. Blood was flying everywhere! One of my Scout buddies became bravely excited. He said, "Come on! Let's get in on the excitement!" He started down the steps, but I grabbed the back of his shirt and said, "No way! The MP's (Military Police) will be here any minute. That is all we need is to get thrown in jail!" We turned around and headed out the door. As we were walking away, the MP's came screeching up with their sirens blaring. My Scout buddy kept thanking me for keeping him out of jail. Besides, all four of us carried side arms. I could just see how that fight was going to turn out! Our pilots squawked at us like chickens! At least we were free chickens! It was nice to get back to our own base camp. We experienced no racial tension at all there. All of this was sure an eye opener for this South Dakota country boy!

Vietnam - African American Vietnam Soldiers Giving the Black Hello

Pugil Sticks

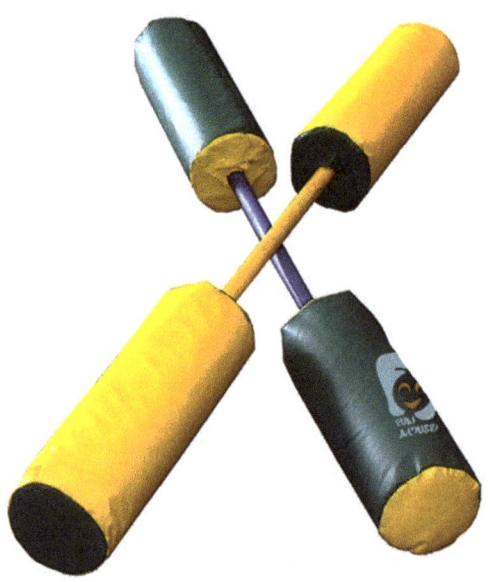

VIETNAM – WOMEN AND CHILDREN ENEMY SOLDIERS

Another Vietnam story that has been on my mind is the ingenuity and hard-working character of the Vietnamese people, both civilians and the enemy. One of the comments that was regularly heard by Vietnam veterans from the American public was we were "Women and Baby Killers!" They were very hurtful words, but they were true.

Many may remember the Court Martial of Lieutenant William Calley that was made public in the late sixties. He was given the order to completely destroy an entire enemy village, including women and children. After the massacre was made public, Lieutenant Calley was thrown under the bus by his commanding officers. What the press did not let the American people know about the Massacre of My Lai, South Vietnam is the legitimate reason for the massacre. Women and children from this village were killing our soldiers! It was very difficult for an American soldier to hurt a woman or a child! The NVA and Viet Cong used this psychology against us very effectively. Until our guys virtually saw the destruction of American soldier lives, did they take killing women and children enemy soldiers seriously. This strategy was ingenious on the part of our enemy.

While out on Hunter/killer Team missions, it was not unusual to spot enemy children and women running to hide in their tunnel and bunker systems to save their lives from our Hunter/killer Team wrath!

We continually would run across the ingenuity of the Vietnamese to use the environment around them to survive. We would come across small streams with fish traps, in cone shape, used to catch fish for their meals. The fish could get in, but they could not get out. The traps would be made of reeds that trapped the fish letting the water continue to run down the stream.

The Vietnamese were very good at taking stuff we, the Americans, discarded or threw out and making something useful out of it. We would throw our used tires and inner tubes away. The Vietnamese would take the tires, cut them into foot sized shape, use the inner tubes for straps, and make sandals. They were called Ho Chi Minh sandals. They were very good, durable sandals. Many of the American soldiers purchased a pair. I had a pair for years until I gave them away.

Since Americans love hamburger sandwiches, the Vietnamese would satisfy the American soldier's appetite for a hamburger and make a profit. However, the hamburger was made from rat or dog! Many soldiers still ate the hamburgers. Not me! Some said it was better than the "C-Rations" (packaged food provided by the military).

The Vietnamese were very hardworking people. The whole family could be seen working in the rice paddies. Our Air Force bombers would take out bridges the enemy needed to transport supplies to their troops and the next week the bridges would be back, being built in a hurry. That is the way it was with anything we destroyed that was built by the enemy. We would burn an enemy village. The following month it would be built back!

Because of my service in Vietnam, my two R&R's to Taipei, Taiwan (Nationalist China, not Communist), and my R&R to Bangkok, Thailand, I grew to love and highly respect the Oriental culture. I love their home-cooked food! In Taipei, Taiwan my tour guide took me to a city where the tour guide's relatives lived. The city was having a special holiday celebration. Our cab could only take us so far, because the streets were closed off packed with celebrating citizens. My mind was blown away when I saw drunken men passed out and staggering all over. I was not expecting to see that in Taiwan.

My guide and I had to walk approximately two miles to the relative's house. I was introduced to a large group of friendly, smiling, family members who opened their arms, hearts, and home to me. There was a large table set with scores of different types of Chinese food. I was invited to help myself. Was that ever a mistake on their part! Being a 25-year-old young man with a country boy appetite, good food was my weakness! Obviously, I could not understand a word that was being said. There was a lot of laughter! My tour guide had to translate for me. They were saying they had not seen anyone eat as much as I did. With that said, the matriarch of the family kept encouraging me to eat on. She was very proud I loved her cooking! What she really did not understand was the crappy food I had to eat in Vietnam. I hope never to have to eat another C-Ration. We did get some hot meals, but the quality was not the best. We had to drink powdered milk that was not quality tasting. It took some getting used to after drinking fresh cow milk growing up. Food is still my weakness, but only if it is really good food!

Ho Chi Minh Sandals

VIETNAM – RELATIONSHIPS WITH THE GUYS!

WITH THIS VIETNAM story I wanted to explore and explain personal relationships among the troops. In my opinion, relationships among troops are different from civilian relationships, especially in a war zone. Because of team work being needed to survive and win battles, a strong brotherhood develops among your fellow platoon members and others in your unit company. One must learn to trust their team members. In our platoon of Scouts, we helped each other become better at our jobs. We shared some information about families and back home, but it was limited.

There was this underlying feeling for me not to get too connected to a fellow soldier in case he was killed in action. It was still very painful (more anger than pain) to lose a fellow team member, but the grieving time had to be short. They were there and now they were gone. Back to battle we had to go! We could not allow any distractions. Not taking the time to properly grieve over the loss of a person you cared about was not a healthy process. It only added to the stress of war. So, I personally tried to keep individual relationships a little distant. I guess that is why I never contacted or received contact from any of the guys I served with in Vietnam after I arrived home.

On August 16, 2018 I had one of my fellow Vietnam War platoon members stop by to visit on his way through my town of Zanesville, Ohio. I, my friend, and our wives visited most of the afternoon and went out to dinner together. We could not help hugging each other hello and goodbye! What a marvelous time we had re-hashing old memories! It felt so good renewing that old kinship we had in Vietnam. You see, he is my Vietnam brother! Vietnam brothers have a special love for each other. But we all held back certain feelings in our relationships so the pain of loss would be not as great. Those that lost their lives killed in action were not talked about a lot. Once on a rare occasion their name would pop up.

In down time many of the guys sat around for hours playing cards. Spades was the most popular card game played in our company. Anytime a group was gathered waiting on anything out came a deck of cards. Otherwise down time was spent reading or sleeping. Sometimes groups were only gathered for drinking beer or smoking marijuana. One could walk outside his hooch and see a group of 50 guys sitting in a large circle smoking marijuana out in the moon light air.

Sometimes to relax and rid ourselves of the stress of war, we flew to the beach. The weather was so hot and humid. Our clothes stuck to our bodies all the time. We went without shirts as much as possible. If we didn't our shirts would be wet with sweat. It was quite refreshing to jump in the cool ocean water to play around for a bit and body surf. Some of us would swim while some stood guard duty and then we would change places! Vietnam has some very beautiful beaches.

Relieving stress helped us do better when we were on missions.

While flying on missions, it was extremely important one's mind be sharp and focused! If a Scout Crew Chief/Gunner was hung over, was drinking, or was high on something, we would not let him fly. Sometimes we would let the pilots fly if they were not hungover too badly. If they were drinking or high on drugs, no flying. We had to be focused!

We would receive intelligence reports of enemy activity in a certain area. It was our job, as Hunter/Killer Teams, to find the enemy and annihilate them from tree top level. As a Scout Crew Chief/Gunner, we had to have the eye sight of an eagle. With the jungle being somewhat thick, we had to be able to spot things that indicated the enemy was in the area. For instance, the enemy hooch's were thatched out of natural growth from the area. Over time with all the rain, humidity, and moisture, the hooch's would start to smell musty and have a mildew smell. We would be flying at tree-top level and I would say to my pilot, "Oh! I smell an enemy village!" We would slow down and look very carefully, flying at treetop level to locate the enemy village. Some of them were hidden very well. If it was a small village, we burned it down ourselves using incendiary grenades. They burned so hot they would start wet hooch's on fire! If the village was a large village and would take us too long to burn down, we would call in an air strike by the Air Force.

The NVA (North Vietnamese Army) used chickens and pigs for food. We would be flying along above the tree tops and I would smell a pig. The pigs like to lay in mud there as they do in the States leaving that pig farm smell. We would stop, look slowly, and sure enough find an enemy village. The same went for chickens. Chickens would start running all over the place from the sound of our helicopters. We could always spot those scurrying chickens. There are two things Vietnam did not discourage me from after I came home! Eating chicken! I love fried chicken! Killing in Vietnam discouraged me from hunting because I just did not want to kill anymore! But chicken and pork? Not a chance! I love my bacon and ham!

Vietnam - Me At The Far Left Shooting BS With The Guys

Vietnam - Relaxed Swimming At The Beach On A Blistering, Hot Day

Vietnamese Hooch (House) Located In The Jungle

Vietnam - Type of Jungle Where We Hunted Enemy Soldiers

VIETNAM – ANTI-WAR DEMONSTRATIONS

ONE OF THE things that was very demoralizing for me and several of my fellow Vietnam soldiers was all the protesting against the Vietnam War at home. Thus meaning, we did not get the emotional support we deserved! My father served in World War II in England as an airplane mechanic. He used to mention on a very rare occasion of the bombing attacks on England by the German Air Force. In fact, I am the result of built up, raging, reproductive hormones released when my father arrived home! He arrived home in 1945. I was born in 1946. My mother kept a framed picture of my Dad's basic training picture, taken in his Army dress uniform, sitting around the house. I remember, as a young boy, admiring that picture viewing my Dad as a war hero. I have always been very patriotic! My brothers and sisters feel the very same as I do about the love and patriotism for our country. It is in our DNA!

As I mentioned in an earlier Vietnam story, I gave a speech in a speech class in college about why we should be in Vietnam. I discovered the shipping lane around the south side of Vietnam was the second most used shipping lane in the world. Whoever controlled South Vietnam controlled that shipping lane and world commerce. I also discovered that South Vietnam was rich in minerals, ores, gas, oil, and timber (etc.). If South Vietnam fell into the hands of Russia and China, who were financing North Vietnam for the spreading of Communism, those resources would give them military strength to use against us. I was convinced we needed to protect South Vietnam from becoming a Communist country that would become our enemy. I would rather fight a war there than here on our homeland endangering our families!

The demonstrations by my generation against the Vietnam War bothered me. I did not feel the same way about the Vietnam War as they did. I had a hard time understanding why the males would go as far as to burn their draft cards. When demonstrators started burning the American flag, that is when I became hurt and really angered. How could anyone disrespect the flag that was the banner of our country and freedoms. Many died defending that flag! In my opinion, they were "mentally spitting" on the graves of the fallen soldiers who sacrificed their lives so we could be free!

I was stationed at Fort Carson, Colorado when four students died at Kent State in Ohio on May 4, 1970. I left for Vietnam July 4, 1970 two months later. Students at Kent State were demonstrating against the Vietnam War. The demonstration started getting out of hand. The Governor, James Rhodes of Ohio, sent in the National Guard with loaded weapons and something went wrong! The National Guard started shooting into the crowd of rioting students. Four students died! Later a hit song was written about "Four Dead In O-H-I-O!"

I recall the picture that graced the newspapers and TV stations of a female student kneeling over her dead male friend wailing in agony because of her grief! I read where that picture won a Pulitzer Prize for photography. I felt anger at the stupidity of students being there in the first place. Why didn't they just stay away and go to class! Four senseless deaths! At the time, I felt the National Guard was doing their assigned duty.

Draft age college students were not the only ones who felt they were being unjustly forced to do something against their will, "Fight in Vietnam!" The predominant religion at the time of the Vietnam War was Buddhism. The religion of Buddhism was being persecuted by the South Vietnamese government. Citizens were beaten and killed for worshiping Buddha. I recall reading about Buddhist Monks lighting themselves on fire in the middle of a well-used street in Saigon (now Ho Chi Minh City) in protest to their mistreatment! Every country has citizens who demonstrate a different way to get their point across.

I admired the South Vietnamese who were dedicated worshipers of Buddha. Not that I agreed with their religion, but because they were dedicated to practicing strongly the religion they believed! I have that respect for anyone who practices their faith with dedication and loyalty even though I do not agree with them. If you believe in something, jump in with your whole self!

I recall, while serving in Vietnam, coming across incense burning in groups where a hooch maid or a prostitute, who had sneaked into our base camp for profit, had been praying to Buddha. When they would hear someone coming, they would quickly disappear. They did not want us to see who was doing the praying! I suspect that came from the fear of the South Vietnamese government persecuting them for worshiping Buddha.

I remember feeling sorrow for these humble, hardworking people who worshiped, in my opinion, a false god. If they only knew the only true and living God, they would have so much more joy and happiness. It is my understanding now, from my reading, that Christianity is getting a strong foothold in South Vietnam!

Civil, peaceful demonstrations are necessary to let those doing the governing know where they are governing in the wrong way. The violence is what bothers me. Violence begets violence! No one wins! Everyone loses! And, in war? The only winners are those that are left!

VIETNAM – THOU SHALL NOT KILL! AM I CONDEMNED?

VIETNAM WAS AN experience that has had an impact on many a Vietnam soldier's life; mine included! It is pretty much a given when a soldier goes into battle, he will kill another human being. I have been able to relate enough of my Vietnam experiences, now, that I feel I can share some of my inner-feelings about taking a life of one of Heavenly Father's children.

You see, I know that He loves you and me unconditionally as does His Son, Jesus Christ, our Savior. That is one regret I have in serving in Vietnam not being more spiritual to be closer to Jesus Christ and Heavenly Father. I was not a religious person when I went to Vietnam. I did not go to church. I had not ever read the Bible. I had never had personal prayer! I believed in God, but that was it! I feel if I had been a true follower of Jesus Christ my Vietnam experiences would have been entirely different. Even though I still would have experienced the horrors of war, my reactions and feelings would have not been so dark!

I came to love going out on a mission to destroy the enemy! It is sort of like the same feeling an avid hunter gets when he goes deer hunting. He cannot wait to get out into the woods to get that trophy deer. That is how I felt about killing the enemy! I came to hate the North Vietnamese and Viet Cong soldiers.

I hunted deer and jack rabbits before I went to Vietnam, but I have not hunted a single day since I have returned home. I just do not want to kill anything anymore! I cannot even bury one of our beloved dogs when they pass away! I have someone else bury them in my pasture where I do not know where they are buried. I do not want to be reminded of death. Funerals are not a comfortable time for me. It is one event I do not like attending, even the funerals of dear friends or family members. It stirs up too many memories! I force myself to attend funerals out of respect for the families on occasion.

I never saw anyone pray or saw any prayer circles or groups while in Vietnam. I never saw anyone reading out of their Bible. I never saw a church gathering or knew of anyplace where others were gathering for church services, impromptu or led by a Chaplain. There probably were some, I just never saw or heard of them!

I do not think I would have participated anyway! God was a far distant being in my life. The world had my heart! When I returned from Vietnam, I was trying to find myself. I was participating in many worldly activities trying to have fun again. On this distinct day I was feeling somewhat down. That was not like me. I have always been a positive, fun loving person. I love joking around. But on this unusual day, my demeanor was at a real low! I was not thinking suicide. That is something I have never thought about! I was just trying to figure out a way to get out of that low spot. Then, the answer popped into my head. Pray! I thought to myself, "Do what?" Pray! I have never prayed in my life, even as a child! I never ever did the "Now I Lay Me Down To Sleep" thing! The more I thought about praying I finally decided to try it. I knelt beside my bed to pray. Now what? I did not even know what to say. Finally, I started having an awkward conversation with Heavenly Father. That was a defining experience in my spiritual healing!

I started to go to church. One of the first things I confessed to my religious leaders was I had violated the sixth commandment of the ten commandments. "Thou Shalt Not Kill!" How was I to be worthy to enter the presence of the Lord after I die with taking the life of one of His children? I was assured the sin was not upon me. I was told the sin was upon those who caused the war and ordered me into battle. I was told about all the wars in the Bible. When God's children would start to pull away from Him, He would stop protecting them from their enemies and they would be attacked and destroyed. Just as when Babylon destroyed Judah and carried the Princes of Judah off to Babylon. Jerusalem was destroyed! I was told how the Israelite's were commanded by God to destroy those who were wicked occupying the Promised Land so His promises to the Israelites would be fulfilled. This knowledge was comforting, but it took a lot of prayer, meditating, and pondering to realize the sin of killing was not upon me. I had to forgive myself.

I read a story a year after I started going to church about two medics who worked in the morgue in Vietnam. Their duty was to clean up the bodies to prepare them to be shipped back to America to be buried. They were each working on a different body on a Sunday when it became time for them to go to their weekly church services gathering. After the services, they returned to their work! One of the medics started to resume cleaning the deceased soldier he had been working on before he went to the church services. The medic noticed a tear rolling down the soldier's cheek! The medic hollered to his coworker,

"Hey! Can dead bodies cry?" His buddy said he did not know. Out of concern, they immediately called a doctor to check this situation out. A heart beat could not be detected before, but now there was a faint heart-beat. The doctor called for help to give this soldier back his life. The medics found out later the soldier was a devout Christian who had been silently praying someone would see he was not dead. He could not speak or move! He could only cry! His faith in God had saved his life!

As I look back on my experiences in Vietnam, I can see blessings! If those experiences had never happened to me, I would probably have not turned my life over to God! To me, that is an awesome blessing! I needed it! I want it! I love it! I love the peace, the spiritual feelings, the joy of service in my church and to others, and I look forward to going to church each and every Sunday! All of this happened 44 years ago to a 28-year-old, single, Vietnam War veteran! I now have no hard feelings! Only hope!

Directions On How To Live My Life...The Holy Bible

VIETNAM – TANKS (AND TANKERS) WERE A VIETNAM WAR BLESSING

THE VIETNAM WAR was a guerilla fought war! Infantry (grunts) and Special Forces were the backbone of winning this war. However, tanks did play an important role in destroying the enemy, especially in supporting the infantry.

My experience with tanks was either from the air, as I was flying on a mission, or when the tank companies would come into the base camps for resupply or rest. We called the people on tanks and personnel carriers "Tankers!" These guys experienced pretty much the same discomfort, fear, and loneliness as the grunts did. The difference was they could hide or sleep inside their tanks or personnel carriers.

The tanks would have their big gun along with a mounted M-50 caliber machine gun and some M-60 machine guns. The personnel carriers usually had an M-50 caliber machine gun mounted on the front and two M-60 machine guns mounted one on each side. To give one the idea how powerful an M-50 caliber machine gun is, sometimes an M-50 caliber machine gun was mounted on a Jeep. These Jeeps were used to accompany truck convoys as chaperones. When they would fire the M-50, it would bounce the Jeep all over the place as if the Jeep was dancing a jig. The bullets from the M-50 would cut sizeable trees in half! Thus, the M-50 caliber machine gun could do some serious damage during an enemy attack.

While flying on missions in Hunter/Killer Helicopter Teams, we would see the tank companies from the air. They provided artillery support for the grunts. From time to time (we would be far off out of firing range) we would see them driving down a road as fast as they could go firing every weapon on the tank they had. The first time I witnessed that, I thought, what the hell! I found out later they were making a "thunder run!" They did this to clear out any mines or booby traps and to flush out any enemy ambushes before a truck convoy would pass through. The tanks usually held up well to mines and booby traps. The "thunder run" would keep going until they either ran out of road or ran low on ammunition.

Other times we would notice them in a large circle with their guns pointed outward. I was told this was "circling up" (like a wagon train). Then, at night they would have a "mad minute" where they would fire everything they had out into the jungle for a minute. They might do this more than once per night depending on the intelligence they had on the enemy movement. The next morning, they would send out armed details to look for dead bodies. The enemy sure did not like this maneuver.

More than once I witnessed tanks or personnel carriers stuck in the mud. Mud was a fact of life for a tanker in our area. I do not ever remember a tanker coming back to base camp who did not have mud all over him.

One of things tankers feared the most was the enemy B-40 rocket. It could either do serious damage to a tank (especially the track system) or destroy a personnel carrier. It made it very dangerous for those inside of either!

I belonged to the 1/10 Air Cav (first of the tenth air cavalry). This battalion consisted of three companies of tanks and one company of helicopters. Because we were part of a cavalry, many of our pilots would wear black cowboy hats with gold bands when not flying. So, the tanks I witnessed from the air, belonged to our battalion. Occasionally, as anything mechanical will do, a tank or personnel carrier would break down and could not be repaired in the field. If the tank was too far from a base camp to be towed by another tank, a Chinook helicopter (sh*t hook) would come lift it out and take it to where it had to be repaired.

Sometimes a tank would be outfitted with a large Roman plow on the front. This tank would be used to clear out brush around a base camp or fire base to make a secure, visible area between the jungle and the wire perimeter of the base camp. Tanks played a very important role in the Vietnam War. They were not sent over in large quantities until 1969. Yes, the North Vietnamese Army had tanks, but I never saw one. I think they were used farther north near the North Vietnam border called the "DMZ" (De-militarized Zone). The northern part of South Vietnam was designated pretty much for the Marines to destroy, but some Army units were there too.

I have a lot of respect for tankers! They sacrificed a lot even though they could get in out of the rain. It was still wet and damp. It was still hot, miserable, and humid. They had to eat C-rations. They could not take baths except for spit baths occasionally. They made an awful big target for the enemy who could easily sneak up on a tank. When that happened, it was extremely hard on the ears. Hearing would be a problem for a few hours. And, there would be casualties. God bless the tankers!

Vietnam - Tanks "Circled Up" To Shoot A Night Time "Mad Minute"

Vietnam - A Tanker's Home Away From Home A Personnel Carrier

Vietnam - One Of Our Battalion Tanks

VIETNAM – THE HO CHI MINH TRAIL

ONE POPULAR NAME that was written and spoken of in the American news media was the Ho Chi Minh Trail, named after the President of North Vietnam, Ho Chi Minh. The trail was used to transport supplies to the North Vietnamese Army (NVA) and the Viet Cong Army fighting in South Vietnam. Being a Communist country, North Vietnam was financed by Communist Russia and Communist China. Most of the weapons and supplies were given to North Vietnam by Russia and China.

The trail started in North Vietnam, ran through parts of Laos and Cambodia, weaving in and back out of South Vietnam. There were times when 3000 to 6000 enemy supply trucks would be on the Ho Chi Minh Trail at one time. They would move at night and many times be camouflaged with jungle brush for day movement to make it harder to spot from the air by U.S. forces! Bicycles were also used to transport supplies. Hundreds of them loaded down with more load than one can imagine would work their way south.

The Ho Chi Minh Trail in the early 70's was bombed so much it left large bomb craters on the trail, making it almost impassable for trucks and bicycles to maneuver the trail. Elephants were used to move enemy supplies! The bomb craters would fill up with rain water making swimming holes for the local village people.

Truck convoys, bicycle groups, and elephant trains would pack supplies to "way stations" established several miles apart. The supplies were off loaded at each way station, reloaded on different trucks, bicycles, or elephants to be sent down the road to the next way station until they arrived at their designated destiny. The U.S. Air Force would bomb enemy "way stations" and bridges trying to stop the enemy from being supplied with ammunition, weapons, and other necessities. When this happened, the "way stations" and bridges would be rebuilt within two weeks or less to be operational again for use.

This was extremely frustrating for the U.S. Military brass! The countries of Laos and Cambodia were cooperating with the North Vietnamese in their war efforts. This presented not only logistical problems for the United States military, but political problems. The U.S. military was not allowed to enter either country. It was finally agreed the U.S. military could bomb the Ho Chi Minh Trail in Laos and Cambodia, but no troops on the ground could enter either of these countries. Even if we did, we would be fighting many militant tribes and militias in each country.

When I arrived at my permanent duty station in Phan Thiet, South Vietnam in late July 1970, my helicopter company had just returned from a mission into Laos. The ARVN (Army of the Republic of Viet Nam) partnered with our helicopter company. We gave air support to them as they went into Laos to attack the enemy forces that would come into South Vietnam on raids and disappear back into Laos to escape being destroyed by our military power. The two-week mission, flown out of Pleiku, South Vietnam, was not very successful. The ARVN had a lot of casualties. They were trained by the American military. They just did not have the heart of the American soldier!

Their country had been at war for decades. Most of the Vietnamese did not even understand or know why they were fighting a war. Many of the Vietnamese who were members of the ARVN (Army of the Republic of Vietnam) joined because it was a job that gave them a living to support their families. They had a lot of desertion problems with their soldiers leaving to go home and be with their families.

As I have said, their hearts were just not in it! Two months later our helicopter company did the same thing in Cambodia. Again, the mission was not very successful. Our pilots and helicopter crews were very discouraged and upset with the lack of commitment from the ARVN. They did not want to follow the instructions of the mission objectives very well. The pilots and crews were used to the heart and soul of the good old American soldier! I was not a flying Crew Chief at that time. I was a Crew Chief for a Cobra Gunship. Only the pilot and co-pilot flew in these helicopters in tandem (one behind the other). My responsibility was ground support. The pilots and crews told me many times how many bomb craters were along the Ho Chi Minh Trail that eliminated enemy truck convoys as they flew over it. Bomb craters was one thing the enemy could not rectify after a bombing. They made good swimming holes, though!

VIETNAM – PUFF, THE MAGIC DRAGON

I MENTIONED IN an earlier story my first duty station was at a place on the South China Sea coast of Vietnam south of Cam Ranh Bay where I entered the country. My MOS (Military Occupational Specialty) was Aircraft Armament Repair which was repairing the weapon systems on a Cobra Gunship. My first assignment was to be a Crew Chief on a Cobra Gunship. I not only repaired and loaded the armament systems, I also took care of the Cobra mechanically.

At one time I was without a Cobra Gunship to be a Crew Chief on, because enemy "Sappers" (enemy special forces) came into our compound disguised as ARVN (Army of the Republic of Viet Nam), which was the South Vietnam army. The Sappers blew up eight of our Cobra Gunships, marched out through the perimeter wire after a path was made by incoming mortar rounds, and disappeared into the night unharmed.

That was a scary, hectic, unorganized night. We lost one of our guys when he took a direct hit from a mortar round while doing guard duty on top of the bunker that was hit. His fellow soldier on guard duty with him was sleeping in the area below the bunker roof. The bunker (made of sand bags) caved in on top of him trapping him there. After listening to his air piercing screams, he was finally uncovered and removed. The soldier never recovered from that. He remained drunk the rest of his tour. It was a very sad situation for such a nice guy. The soldier that was killed was his best buddy. They only found pieces of him.

One day all the Cobra Gunships were scrambled out. The neighboring base camp, about forty miles away, was getting overrun by the Viet Cong (called a suicide attack) in the middle of the day and they needed help fast. The Cobra Gunships kept coming back in for hours to re-arm their weapons. As we rushed to reload them, the pilots informed us there were at least 1000 Viet Cong soldiers. They described the scene as ants on an anthill. Normally, the enemy soldiers would get high on opium so they would be brave and fearless. They just keep coming and coming, stepping over the dead bodies before them, trying and hoping to breach the perimeter of the base camp to finally overrun it. They were getting close to overcoming our troops. Additional air power was needed. They called for Puff, the Magic Dragon.

Puff, the Magic Dragon was a C-130 cargo plane that had 10 to 20 mini-guns installed, each gun putting out 6000 rounds per minute. When Puff made a pass, they could cover every square inch of a football field. Our pilots hovered off in the distance to watch Puff at work. They described the scene as looking down and seeing a farmer with a sickle-bar-mower mowing long grass down for hay.

Puff, the Magic Dragon made four passes and went home. The Cobra Gunships cleaned up to make sure the base camp was not under any more threat. The Viet Cong came back in the middle of the night to haul their dead away. I never did hear what our casualties were, but I know there were some. We did not lose any pilots. All I know is I sure handled a heck of a lot of ammunition and rockets that day. I was one tired puppy!

VIETNAM – THE AIR FORCE HAD IT MADE!

VIETNAM WAS A breeding ground for new military tactics. Guerilla warfare using helicopters and jets was not a familiar tactic for modern warfare. Our present Army Rangers, Army Special Forces, Navy Seals, Air Force Special Forces, and Marine Special Ops Teams are all learning from the mistakes and successes of fighting in Vietnam.

In my opinion, the Air Force had it made! They had air-conditioned barracks, night clubs, golf courses, libraries with every kind of book and music, excellent food in their dining halls, and big, thick mattresses to sleep on. Our mattresses were little, skinny things.

Being a helicopter company, we had the means of flying to the nearest Air Force base, snatch what we needed, and sneak back out to our home base camp. Sometimes, we would trade NVA war memorabilia for stuff. The military guys in the rear craved that memorabilia. I guess it was their way of saying, "We were there!" We all had Air Force mattresses to sleep on. That added a lot of comfort to our life! The Air Force was our partner in battle. Sometimes, we would come across an enemy village that was big enough it would take our team too long to burn or blow it up. We would call in an air strike. The jets would dive in, drop their bombs, and we got to witness huge, monstrous, explosive clouds. They would normally only have to make one dive! When we flew back in to assess the damage, everything would look like a tornado on steroids had come through.

That was quite a sight for this country boy! The closest bomb I had ever been to, prior to Vietnam, was a cherry bomb on 4th of July. I found out a cherry bomb will blow up a toilet, if a guy throws one down the toilet.

Helicopter gunships sort of evolved over the Vietnam War years. The first gunships were called Charlie Gunships. They were a sized down slick (kind of like the difference between a two-door car and a four-door car) with rocket pods or miniguns on each side. The Cobra Gunship was developed and replaced the Charlie Gunship. The enemy feared them both. The NVA and the VC would run as fast as they could to find a tunnel or bunker because their lives depended on it. We called them "sh*t runs" because the sh*t was being scared out of them!

The rockets had little steel flechettes (a nail sized, steel arrow) inside them. When the rocket exploded, the steel flechettes would fly every which direction. Today the Cobra Gunship has been replaced by the Apache Gunship. The Apache Gunship (with all its advanced technology) is far superior to the Cobra Gunship.

Vietnam - Cobra Gunship Armed With Rockets Pods and Minigun

Vietnam - Cobra Gunship Firing Rockets

Vietnam - Charley Gunship (Before the Cobra Gunship)

Vietnam - Air Force Mattress

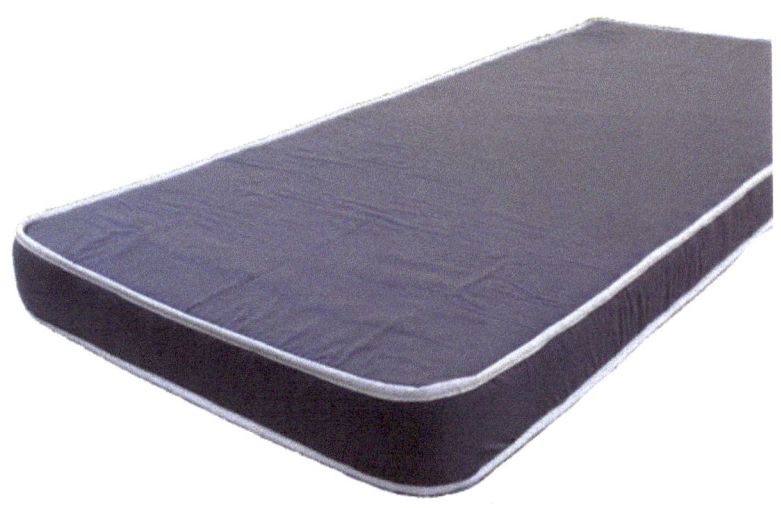

Vietnam - Air Force Golf Course During Vietnam War
See What I Mean By Having It Made?

VIETNAM ENTERTAINMENT – VIETNAMESE ROCK BAND AND GO-GO GIRLS

THE STRESS OF war is hard to feel or understand unless one has been in war. The stress is immense. Our company commander at the time, who was the rank of major, decided the company needed to unwind. He hired a Vietnamese band that played American rock music, go-go dancers, and a deuce and half truck loaded with ladies of the evening. Because of the respect our Scout team received from the rest of our company, they always reserved front row seats for us at any event we attended. I along with my fellow Scouts hooted, hollered, danced in place, and stuck dollar bills in the go-go dancers' bikini bottoms to keep them dancing dirty. It was a blast that let us relieve a bunch of stress. The medic station received an increase in patients in the next two weeks giving shots to those who contacted VD (Venereal Disease) from the ladies of the evening. That was three days of penicillin shots, one in each butt cheek on alternating days. Guys complained about not being able to sit down because of the soreness. Can't you just feel sorry for them?

Back to after the event. In the back of my mind, I was concerned that some of the civilian Vietnamese that were let inside our company area for the event might be working for the enemy.

After the band quit playing and the festivities died down, I spent the rest of the night wandering along the perimeter of our company area and among our helicopters with my weapons of war making sure (in my mind) we were not going to be surprised by an enemy attack.

In the evenings before dark the infantry guys would go out into the wired perimeter to check all the Claymore explosives to make sure they were turned the right way. A Claymore is a curved explosive mine about a foot long packed with C-4 explosives and 720 little ball bearings. When they exploded, they did a lot of lower body damage. During the day, sometimes a hooch maid (cleaning lady) would sneak out into the wire and turn the Claymores back towards our direction. They did this because the enemy was threatening to kill their families. Therefore, the grunts had to check the wire out every evening to make sure the claymores were turned the right direction.

While I was in Camp Kue Army Hospital in Okinawa, the soldier in the bed next to mine had been wounded when one of his squad accidentally tripped a Claymore while they were checking Claymores in the wire. It took all the meat and muscle off his lower legs from the knee down to the ankle. All one could see in that area were his lower leg bones. I watched the doctor dress and clean that wound for many days on end. Sometimes the doctor would ask me to hold something for him. I really felt for this soldier. He was so drugged up, he slept most of the time. When he was awake, he and I would talk. That is how I knew what happened to him. The doctor did not want to cut his lower legs off. They were trying to save them. I was sent back to Vietnam, so I do not know the results of his medical care.

Working on wounded soldiers was tough on the doctors. They wanted so badly to save lives and help soldiers heal from their wounds. One morning I had an appointment for a checkup with my surgical doctor. When I walked into his office, I could see he had been crying. I asked him what was wrong. He told me he had lost a patient that morning. He had done surgery a couple of weeks earlier on a soldier who had been hit in the gut with an enemy grenade. The doctor had been in surgery with him for 22 hours trying to remove all the shrapnel to save the soldier's life. The Army even flew the soldier's elderly parents to Okinawa, because the soldier was in such critical condition. The surgery was successful! The soldier started to improve to the point where the parents felt comfortable in flying back home. They were still on the plane trip home when their son passed away. I really felt for this doctor! I could not help but give him a hug and tell him he was the greatest doctor in the world. He thanked me for that. God bless all the medical personnel who work to make soldiers and veterans whole again!

Vietnam - Damn! What a Go-Go Girl! Go Girl!

Vietnam - Claymore Mine, Clacker (Detonator Switch), and Wiring

Vietnam - Wire Perimeter Barrier (Concertina Wire)

VIETNAM - BROKEN HEART

AS I HAVE mentioned in earlier stories, there is a lot of stress, anger, and loneliness in a war zone. When there was mail call, I never have seen so many faces brighten up as they received their mail and packages from home. It was a joy to experience. Unfortunately, not all news from home was good.

I walked into my hooch one afternoon, after flying a combat mission, to witness one of my fellow platoon members and Scouts sobbing and sobbing! I put my weapons down, rushed over to him, and said, "Buddy (I have left names out of my stories on purpose because I have not obtained permission to use them). What in the world is the matter?" He handed me the papers he had received in the mail. This kid was only 18 years old when he came to Vietnam, now just turning 19. He had married his high school sweetheart a few weeks before being shipped out to Vietnam. She had sent him divorce papers. I was crushed! I never wanted to choke a woman to death as much as I wanted to choke that woman for tearing out the heart of my friend. I grabbed my buddy, hugged him with all the love I could give him, and told him we would help him work through this pain. All he would do prior to this divorce was talk about his wife! He loved her dearly, but his heart was smashed!

He made it through the next few months with the help and support of our platoon. Keeping him busy helped a lot. I have another acquaintance who left behind a fiancée when he left for Vietnam. They wrote extremely, mushy, love letters to each other often. This guy could not wait to get home and hold her in his arms. She was waiting at the airport when he arrived home, waiting with his parents, and some of his buddies. The scene was emotional and filled with kisses and hugs. Then, one of his buddies pulled him aside and told him his fiancée was living with another man. He wanted to knock his buddy on his butt. He did not believe it. He found out later it was true. He started drinking very heavily for months after that.

War is tough enough on soldiers, but to destroy them emotionally like that is cruel and unusual punishment. These men had forgiving hearts after time, but it was very difficult for them to forgive. Luckily, in most cases, time heals the heart. I think many Vietnam veterans have forgiven much!

Every time I saw one of my war buddy's cry, I cried with them inside. I was a hardened warrior. I could not let others see me cry openly. Sometimes I would lay in my bunk at night with tears rolling down my cheeks. No one saw those tracks of tears. No one! I had to show stability! I had to stay focused! I had to be hardened in heart to survive! Many of us were like that. The enemy was not going to win! Damn it! I was going home and alive in one piece! I could show no weakness! Weakness caused one to be killed! I am home, aren't I?

Luckily over the last 48 years I have slowly learned to openly cry. I don't know if it is really crying, but I get a lump in my throat and tears in my eyes. This happens when I read or see a sad story or maybe a story with a real joyful, happy ending. I catch myself crying during movies. Sometimes I cry when a certain song is played. Sometimes I cry when I sing or listen to certain hymns. Sometimes I cry when I bear my testimony of my belief in Jesus Christ and my gratitude for Him. Sometimes I cry when others are really hurting physically, mentally, or spiritually.

Writing stories of my Vietnam War experiences has really brought out my crying! Crying has really helped me to cleanse my deepest, hidden pains of the memories of the Vietnam War and how I was treated when I arrived home. The healing has happened! I must give thanks to those who knowingly or unknowingly have helped lift my Spirit to new heights of joy! That is why I have written this book! I want all Vietnam Veterans who are not healed yet to come out of the Vietnam War closet! Come cry with me! Start by writing your experiences down! Cry your heart out! It will take time, but your soul will soar! I give you my word on it!

Vietnam - Mail Call! Happy Time in a War

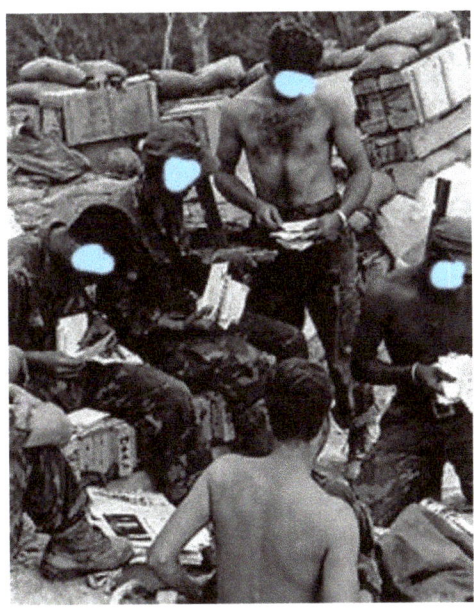

VIETNAM – THE GRUNT'S WAR

IN VIETNAM, IN my opinion, the hardest job was to be a grunt (infantryman). Before I was drafted in May 1969, I had worked for two logging seasons in Alaska. The second season I was there (1968), a young man came out to our logging camp who had just returned home from Vietnam for a 30-day leave. He was bored, came out to our logging camp for something to do, and ended up working on my logging crew. I had a lot of time to talk with him! He was a grunt! After listening to his Vietnam War experiences, I absolutely decided I did not want to be a grunt!

I extended for a year at the beginning of my basic training to get a training school that would keep me from becoming a grunt. I extended my enlistment from two years to three years. My Momma did not raise any fool! Grunts had the hardest job of all in Vietnam.

They would be out humping the bush for weeks at a time trying to destroy Charlie (enemy Vietnamese). They might, if they were lucky, make it back into their base camp once a month. Not only did they have to fight the enemy, they had to fight wetness from the rain; they had to fight wetness from the heat and humidity, they had to fight mud and water; they had to fight rashes and foot rot because they were never dry or could bathe; they had to fight the mosquitoes and the malaria, they had to fight heat exhaustion; they had to go weeks with wet, dirty clothes and socks (if they wore socks); they had to go weeks without a hot meal eating C-rations (not good); they had to fight loneliness and no mail call until they returned to base camp; they had to fight depression, frustration, and fear. When they did get back to base camp, they might get two or three days of hot showers, hot meals, a cold beer, and mail call! There might even be some donuts there left by the Red Cross girls called "Donut Dollies."

Back out humping the bush the grunts were constantly being haunted by booby traps. Booby traps were a major killer or cause of wounds in Vietnam! Some of the booby traps were trip wires attached to enemy grenades under the muddy water in a rice paddy the grunts would have to cross. A square pit would be dug with long, sharp, skinny sticks in it called punji sticks. They were placed across the bottom of the pit with human waste or snake poison on them. The pit would then be covered with light ground cover that looked like the rest of the trail. The grunt would come along, step on the light ground cover, step or fall into the pit, and the punji sticks would pierce their feet and body!

Grenade booby traps were also used along the trail! The enemy were experts at setting booby traps to maim or kill our grunts. Over time our grunts learned from the enemy and set their own booby traps for the enemy or once an enemy booby trap was located, they would move it so the enemy would not know where it was.

Another thing, grunts had to deal with was the enemy's elaborate tunnel system they used for hiding and for surprise attacks. The enemy's strategy was to strike fast to do as much killing and wounding of our grunts as possible! Then disappear as quickly as they appeared! By the time the enemy was located for our grunts to kill, they were gone. This is guerilla warfare! Sometimes the enemy would be in a tunnel hiding and hear the grunt patrol walk over the tunnel. When the grunts had passed by, the enemy would pop out of a tunnel opening that was camouflaged, surprise the grunts, wound or kill some, and then disappear into the tunnel system.

This type of enemy had to be killed! So, grunts would be assigned to go into the enemy tunnels to destroy the enemy. Usually, the smaller grunts were the ones who had to follow the enemy into their tunnels. The NVA and VC were not very big in stature. Oriental people are normally not big in size.

These grunts were called "Tunnel Rats." I shake with fear every time I visualize a "Tunnel Rat" going into an enemy tunnel. Not only did they have to worry about being killed by the enemy, it was very dark! Then, they had to worry about punji stick booby traps, enemy grenade booby traps, and sometimes poisonous snakes that were used as booby traps. "Tunnel Rats" were considered "nuts" by me! They were some-kind-of maximum brave!

The grunts always talked about a poisonous snake in Vietnam they called a "step-and-a-half. Once one was bitten, they had a step and a half to go before they died! I never saw one, but I heard the grunts talk about them, especially the "Tunnel Rats" (I personally think "Tunnel Rats" were psychological)! Some say the step-and-a-half snake was actually a myth told to the grunts by the brass so they would be extra careful around any poisonous snake. I sure as heck believed one would die in a step and a half if bitten.

The grunts had to deal with tigers! Many a grunt told me how scary a tiger's scream is in the middle of the night. It is even worse when all you see is eyes in the night. I never talked to a grunt who liked to go into triple canopy jungle. This is jungle with three layers of foliage. Inside it was dark and full of eye balls! I don't care how many scary movies you can sit through, triple canopy jungle, as well as the enemy tunnels, would destroy your bravery!

Tigers from time to time would stalk a Vietnamese village. Sometimes villagers were killed by a tiger. That is when villagers would organize a hunting party to kill the predator. That man-eating tiger had a taste for human blood which made the tiger even more dangerous! The tiger had to be killed!

The news media always reported when Bob Hope went to Vietnam over the Christmas holidays with his USO (United Service Organization) tour. Unfortunately, they usually could not go to the areas where the war dragged on day in and day out. The USO tours usually ended up at the large base camps in the rear that were more secure. Most grunts did not get to see them. When they did, it was a great stress release outlet!

Sadly, due to stress, fear, loneliness, and the need to unwind, some of the grunts would resort to drugs as an outlet. Marijuana was the most common, but heroin and opium became popular because of the availability and the extremely low cost. A huge freezer bag full of marijuana cost $5! A vial of heroin, the size on one's thumb that was 98% pure, sold for $5! Opium varied in price depending on the opium den one went to in the village outside the base camp, but it was cheap.

To stop some of the opium usage problems the military made

many of the villages off limits! If the MP's (Military Police) caught an American soldier in the village, he or she would be arrested. There were a lot of grunts that would buy extra whatever drug and take it into the field with them. Large numbers of grunts had to be sent through drug rehabilitation centers before they could come home. It was cold turkey rehab! No helping drugs!

Can you blame the grunts who were coming home needing that hero's welcome and medical treatment for all their issues and not getting any of it? I am here to tell you the pain goes deep for many of these great men and women. That hero's welcome would have been the "Balm of Gilead" for all these veterans, especially the grunts! It never happened!

Vietnam - Captured Enemy Soldiers Waiting To Be Picked Up

*Vietnam - Slick Helicopter In An LZ
(Landing Zone) Picking Up Grunts*

Vietnam - Door Way Punji Stick Booby Trap

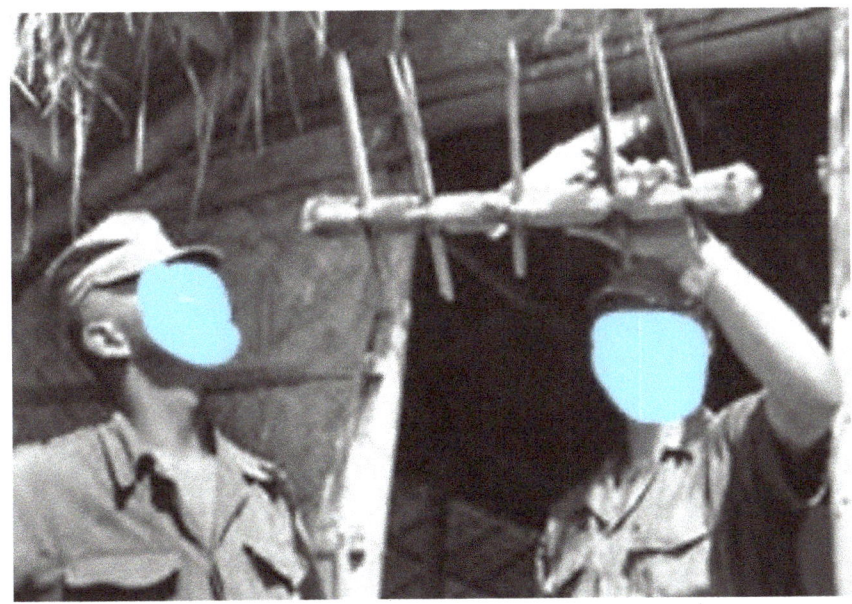

*Vietnam - Grunts Being Inserted
(Unloaded) In A LZ (Landing Zone)*

*Grunts Being Extracted (Pulled Out)
After Humping All Day Looking For NVA*

VIETNAM – PAIN IN THE BUTT SAPPERS!

IN VIETNAM THE most respected enemy soldiers were the North Vietnamese Army (NVA) and Viet Cong (VC) Sappers. They were the rangers or commandos for their army. They were put through months of specialized and intense training. They became skilled in map reading, orienteering (using a compass), booby trap removal, explosives and demolition, tunneling, along with evading and escaping. The purpose of the Sappers was to penetrate American defensive perimeters in advance of an attack by the other NVA or VC. The Sappers would initiate the battle within the perimeter by creating havoc and confusion with explosives in satchel charges at the same time another NVA or VC unit would attack the Americans from outside the perimeter. This tactic used by the Sappers was usually very successful.

The thing unique about the Sappers is they would be nearly naked because clothing would get caught on the concertina wire that was used to help secure the perimeters of the American compounds as they were crawling under the wire. Because Sappers were so good at not being seen crawling through our perimeter wire, the soldiers pulling guard duty would fire off flares every few minutes in the night to see if they could spot any Sappers. The problem was the Sappers could hear the flares go off before they lit up the night sky giving them the opportunity to become motionless and evasive. At Phan Thiet, my first duty station in Vietnam, an ARVN (Army of the Republic of Vietnam) compound and a ROK (Republic of Korea) compound were adjacent to our compound. The Sappers came into our compound during the day disguised as ARVN, stayed until night time, and blew up eight of our Cobra Gunships. They all escaped without any of them getting wounded or killed! That is why we respected them so much!

We had enemy soldiers surrender and come to our side. Their lives were much easier, they were paid better, and they got to make friends with us. These surrendered prisoners were called by different names depending on the unit one served in.

When I was stationed at Phan Thiet, the Viet Cong soldier who helped our ARP's (Aero Rifle Patrol) when they went out in the jungle and rice paddies to hump was called a "Kit Carson Scout!" Some units called these turncoats "Chieu Hoi" (Chew Hoy) which means "with open arms" or "I surrender." Some of them were called "Tiger Scouts." We called our NVA turncoats "Benedict Arnold" after the Revolutionary War General, Benedict Arnold, who became a traitor to General Washington and the colonists by giving secrets to the British. He was caught and executed.

Our Benedict Arnold's name was Tre (pronounced Tree). He was a former Sapper (Special Forces) for the NVA. Having him on our side was such a blessing. When we would be on a mission covering the ARP's out in the jungle, Tre would be considerably ahead of the ARP's locating booby traps. When we hovered over him, he would immediately stop, look up at us, smile, and wave. He wanted to make sure we did not mistake him for the enemy!

Tre and I used to have conversations a lot. I asked him about his Sapper training all the time. Because of Tre giving me knowledge of his training, we were able to discover a jungle NVA Sapper Training School. It may have been one Tre trained at. It looked a lot like what he described to me. That find was a major blessing for us. We destroyed the school, setting the NVA training of Sappers back several months.

I kept asking Tre how good he was. He kept telling me he could come through our wire perimeter in the middle of the day and I would not see him. I told him he was spewing feces from the south end of a bull. He had to ask me what I meant by that. I said, "Bull Sh*t!" He did not like that. I said, "Okay, prove it! Go out and come through our wire perimeter. I will let the guys on guard duty know what is going to happen, so they don't blow you away."

Tre consented. He walked out into the jungle with just a pair of Vietnamese shorts on. He told us the general area he would be coming through an area that covered 75 to 100 yards in width. We sat there concentrating watching the wire from the guard tower, we were in, trying to spot him. We never did see him. About an hour later we heard someone coming up the ladder of the guard tower. Hell! It was Tre! I did not think he could come through our wired perimeter in the middle of the day without being seen. The undergrowth was about a foot high, but you would think one could see the undergrowth move as Tre crawled through it. Tre sure taught me a lesson! That really gave me even more respect for the Sappers. It also made me more paranoid of them coming through our wired perimeter at night. It caused us to re-think some strategies, especially on guard duty.

The NVA and VC used the Russian-made AK-47. It was an automatic weapon that was very reliable in jungle warfare. Grunts would steal an AK-47 when they captured an enemy soldier. They did not have to clean their weapon as often. With all the mud plus water the grunts encountered, they would have to stop and clean their M-16's, especially if they crossed a river or body of water where their weapon would get soaked. They did not have to do that with an AK-47. The grunts that used an AK-47 had to also steal AK-47 ammunition. AK-47 ammunition was the same caliber as our M-60 machine gun ammunition, but not interchangeable. M-60 machine gun ammunition would explode when used in an AK-47 causing injury to the user. Many company leaders would not let their men use AK-47's for that reason. They even had to be cautious when they picked up an enemy AK-47 because of it might be booby trapped.

Some of the most skilled helicopter pilots in Vietnam were the "Dust-Off Pilots" (medical)! They had to land a large helicopter (Slick) in a tight (very small) LZ (Landing Zone), get in quickly, and get out just as quickly to get the wounded to medical help back at the base camp. They also had to have the nerves of steel and guts made of stone. It was not unusual for them to have to land in a hot LZ (bullets and explosives all over the place). Everyone (especially the grunts) had huge respect for the "Dust-Off Pilots." They relied heavily on the Slick crew chief (who was a door gunner on the left side) and the door gunner (who was door gunner on the right side) to guide the pilot in and out of an "LZ" (Landing Zone) while firing their door guns. They would talk to the pilot through the radio system in the helicopter saying, "Clear up right or clear down right or clear up left or clear down left or clear at rear." The crew chief and door gunner were the eyes for the pilots.

There was a short period of time where my company had to live in tents. Because my being in Vietnam in July 1970 through November 1971, base camps were built up enough where tent dwelling was not needed. When the military sent the 4th Division home from An Khe, we were homeless for a short time until they could assign us to another army division. Tents were our home. Believe me, tent dwelling in Vietnam was not like staying in a tent while camping at home. With it being so hot and humid in Vietnam, tents were like ovens. They would not cool down until early in the morning. Then, they would heat up again. Even with fans, tents were unbearable. We did not nap in our own bunk during the day. The Army and Marines who served in Vietnam in the early years of the war all slept in tents, if they did not sleep outside.

During our down time when we were not flying missions, it was very easy to catch us standing or sitting around shooting the BS! One of my fellow Scouts was from England. I met him in AIT (Advanced Individual Training) at Aberdeen Proving Grounds, Maryland. He was a couple of class cycles behind me. He was drafted because he was working in United States on a green card. That made him eligible for the draft. My dad served in England during World War II. He referred to an English man as a limey! So, I nicknamed my English friend "Limey." Everyone called him that. I knew him for almost six months when he told me one day that if we were in England and I called him "Limey," he would have decked me! He went on to explain that limey was an offensive word to be called in England. English sailors in the old days were called limeys because they ate fresh lime (fruit) while at sea to keep from getting scurvy. Limey said he understood we did not realize limey was a derogatory word. I do not think most of the guys really knew his real first name. Limey grew to love us calling him that.

Remember I told you in an earlier story Vietnam Veterans were called "women and baby" killers when we arrived home? One of the guys in our platoon was walking along and heard some animal crying noise. He stopped, looked around, and discovered the noise was coming from a group of puppies that were stuck in a storm drain going under the dirt road that ran through the company area. He hollered for help. Our hooch emptied with everyone wondering what the problem was. Upon learning there were little puppies stuck in this storm drain, everyone made the commitment to get those puppies out.

After much deliberation and failed attempts to pull them out, it was decided the road had to be dug up. Out came the shovels. The hard road was pick axed and dug up, the storm drain opened, and six rescued, grateful puppies cuddled whoever was holding them (everyone wanted to hold one of them). All of us swore they would never be given to the Vietnamese to be made into hamburger. How about those big hearts, huh? Does that sound like monsters who kill women and babies?

Vietnam - Captured Enemy AK-47

*Vietnam – Scout LOACH Destroyed
A By Sapper Satchel Charge*

*Vietnam - Slick Helicopter Destroyed
By A Sapper Satchel Charge*

*Vietnam - Dust-off Helicopter Used
That Carried The Wounded and Dead*

Vietnam - Culvert With Puppies Stuck Inside

Vietnam - Puppies Rescued From the Culvert Going Under the Road

VIETNAM – THE SAGA OF HAMBURGER HILL

PRIOR TO MY arriving in Vietnam the American press told the story of the battle of "Hamburger Hill" in A Sau Valley (pronounced Awe Shaw Valley by us. Pronounced A̲ Saw Valley by those who were there). This battle was where the American military forces, at huge casualty costs, fought for ten days to capture Hill 937. It was called that because the mountain was listed as Hill 937 (937 meters - 3074 feet - above sea level) on the military maps. This was the biggest mountain in that area. It also was covered with double and triple canopy jungle, dense thickets of bamboo, and tall elephant grass. It was a great place for the enemy to hide! It was extremely difficult to maneuver in this difficult terrain. The locals called Hill 937 "the mountain of the crouching beast."

From December 1968 until May 1969 (when I was drafted) I worked in the oil fields of Wyoming living in Newcastle, Wyoming. I recall watching the newscasts of the battle about Hamburger Hill. They showed the grunts trying to work their way up Hill 937. It down-poured rain at one time during the ten-day battle. The news media showed the 101st Airborne Division dealing with the mud taking two steps up the hill and sliding two steps back. They also showed and reported all the casualties caused during this battle. The news media reporting was extremely negative. It was being described as one of the worst battles in the war (the worst one for the 101st Airborne Division was at Dak To in the Central Highlands in November 1967 according to historical reports). The news media criticized the military for fighting a battle that took so many lives and wounded so many of our soldiers. The worst criticism came when the news media found out taking Hill 937 had no strategical worth. A few weeks after the battle of Hamburger Hill ended, Hill 937 was abandoned. The worst part of all the news media negative hype was they brushed over the fact the 101st Airborne Division kicked butt! They destroyed the best the NVA (North Vietnamese Army) had! The NVA casualties were several hundred more than American casualties. The news media had a narrative that we should get out of Vietnam and go home. So, that is how they reported the war.

When I arrived in Vietnam, the battle of Hamburger Hill and the casualties suffered by the American military forces had become legendary. The 101st Airborne Division earned a hero's reputation. Those grunts were admired for their guts and stamina to go back up Hill 937 each and every day knowing some of them would not make it or have to be carried back down the mountain, being wounded.

The battles that took place in the A Sau Valley were the greatest and highest resistance given by the enemy North Vietnamese Army (NVA) up to that point. Hill 937 was only 1.2 miles from the border of Laos. This provided a safe-haven for the NVA when they slipped over the border to get away. The American military could not enter Laos to pursue this evasive and highly trained guerilla army because of politics.

The battle of Hamburger Hill (dubbed "Hamburger Hill" by the fighting soldiers because they were cut down and chopped up like hamburger) was one of the worst fatalities and wounded losses of the war. Sixty percent of the Army forces there were either killed or wounded! When the news media got wind of this battle going on, they rushed to cover the carnage. Because this battle from May 10, 1969 to May 20, 1969 (10 days) was reported on TV and in the newspapers back in the States, the attitude and demonstrations against the Vietnam War took a very negative turn in the minds of the American people and the minds of the politicians. As a result, when I arrived at Cam Ranh Bay, South Vietnam July 5, 1970, our support from back home by America was literally gone!

The A Sau Valley was occupied by the best of the best of the North Vietnamese Army. The Marines tried desperately to clean out A Sau Valley of NVA soldiers. They could not do it. The Marine casualty rate was too high. The Intelligence reports revealed the Hill 937 was occupied by a regiment of NVA. An aggressive Army general wanted to capture that mountain! Stories of Hamburger Hill and other battles in the A Sau Valley spread like wild fire throughout the military in Vietnam. A Sau Valley gained the reputation as being the most dangerous area in Vietnam for our soldiers. Can you imagine arriving in Vietnam as a new guy and finding out you were being assigned to a unit in the A Sau Valley? I suspect a lot of those soldiers were thinking their chances of making it home were slim to none! It was scary to think a general would allow so many casualties. Even with the reputation and admiration the 101st Airborne Division earned, the battle of "Hamburger Hill" put a negative cloud over all of us in Vietnam at that time. It really worried me that some general would try the same thing with us! Fortunately for us, the military leadership had learned their lesson. No general, after that, wanted to jeopardize his career advancement by having a casualty loss as the battle of "Hamburger Hill" had, even though a great battle had been won. With all the brutal resistance the NVA gave the American forces in A Sau Valley, I guess I cannot blame the U.S. Military generals feeling they needed to defeat the pesky NVA occupying the valley. Generals, probably trained in conventional warfare and not understanding guerilla warfare, were trying to defeat an enemy (highly skilled in guerilla warfare) with conventional warfare techniques. They did not work! Even though the Air Force bombed all over the place and the Army artillery lit up the hillsides with holy terror, the enemy still was not affected that much. They had embedded deep into their elaborate bunker and tunnel systems. Then at night they would sneak over into Laos to rest and recuperate. I think if I would have been the general in charge of the Hamburger Hill battle, I would have soaked the whole area with Agent Orange, took my men to the beach for a while to play and rest, and let Agent Orange destroy the enemy. If enough Agent Orange was sprayed, it would have made the NVA extremely sick causing death!

Many families are without their sons, brothers, cousins, uncles, fathers, and neighbors. The sins of this war are not on these individuals! The sins of this war are on the generals and politicians who sent them to war. God bless those brave and honorable soldiers! All those dead soldiers' names are on the Vietnam War Wall Memorial in Washington, DC. I remember how emotional it is for me to visit that memorial! The last time I was in Washington DC with a good friend, he wanted to visit the Vietnam War Wall Memorial. I sat off to the side a short distance for about an hour while he absorbed the impact this wall has on its visitors. I just did not want to go through all those emotions again! It was very impressive for me to also visit the "Tomb of the Unknown Solder!" Both are a must see visit if you are ever in Washington, DC. If either one of these monuments does not stir up your deep-felt patriotism and put a lump in your throat, I do not know what will! Live on in spirit, brothers! (Information on the battle of Hamburger Hill was taken from Historynet.com, Wikipedia, and Warhistoryonline.com).

Vietnam - North Vietnamese Army (NVA) Grave Yard

Vietnam War Wall Memorial in Washington, DC

Vietnam War Memorial Wall Statistics

There are 58,267 names on the wall.
39,996 were 22 or younger.
8,283 were 19. 33,103 were 18.
12 were 17 years old.
5 soldiers were 16.
There are 3 sets of fathers and sons on the wall.
31 sets of parents lost two of their sons.
997 were killed the first day in Vietnam.
1,448 were killed the last day they were in Vietnam.
8 women are on the wall, nurses.
244 Vietnam War soldiers were awarded the Medal of Honor during the war and 153 of their names are on the wall.

Vietnam War Memorial Statues In Washington, DC

VIETNAM NEWS – THE STARS AND STRIPES NEWSPAPER

NEWS WAS NOT plentiful to us where I was stationed. In some areas, particularly in the rear and in the populated areas of Vietnam, news was more readily available because of TV, radio, and newspapers. Our main news source was the military newspaper, The Stars and Stripes. I, like most Americans, trusted and believed the news, whether it came over the airwaves or in print. But I had an unusual experience in Vietnam with the news media.

One day I was reading the Stars and Stripes (it was several weeks old) when I came across an article about a battle I had experienced. As I read this article, I became more and more confused. This is not the way this battle happened! I was there! Why did this battle get misrepresented in the news? This experience planted the first "seeds of doubt" in my believing the main stream media.

When I returned home from Vietnam, I finally realized why America did not welcome home Vietnam Veterans with open arms. So much of the news media reporting on Vietnam was negative, it swayed the opinions and feelings the American people had about the Vietnam War. What most of the American people do not realize is, the Vietnam War could have easily been won. The military of the United States is the best in the world! There are no better soldiers than American soldiers! They fully understand what freedom is and recognize it is worth fighting and dying for. However, the politicians got in the way with their stupid policies.

The military knows how to win wars if the politicians would keep their nose out of military business. But realism is realism! I mentioned in an earlier story I agreed with our being in Vietnam because of the research I did in college to give a speech for a speech class final grade. With all the natural resources, ores, and uranium in South Vietnam and the importance of the shipping lane around the tip of South Vietnam, I did not want all of this to fall in the hands of Russia and China, who were financing and supporting the North Vietnamese Army. I would rather fight a war there than here at home.

One of the stupid policies implemented while I was in Vietnam, was not to fire upon the enemy unless fired upon first. That is like saying, thank you for the kiss before you get the kiss! I was coming home alive, bar none! I am sorry to say I never obeyed that order. This policy was forced upon our military leadership by the politicians.

With all these experiences with the news media, I wonder now, how many articles I have read or heard, and believed, were actual, unbiased news reporting? Were the articles leaning towards the biased opinion of the reporter? I guess only the reporter can answer that.

In today's real world one needs to check news sources from several different sources. I get my news from TV, radio, several internet sites, both liberal and conservative, and on social media.

Somewhere lies the truth. It gives me input from both sides of an issue that helps me arrive to a conclusion. The news media is so important to preserving our freedoms by outing corruption in our government: local, state, national, and international. The news media is also important to the happiness and wellbeing of its readers and listeners by reporting the feel good and uplifting news that gives us hope. The news media is also important to warn us about weather and crimes that surround us. The news media certainly has its place in our lives. I am truly grateful for it. Nevertheless, I have to say the news media played a major part in the very poor treatment Vietnam veterans received, by the American people, when they arrived home. I am so happy the news media has repented! They now pay such wonderful tributes to those who have served and are serving in the military today. Thank you, news media!

VIETNAM – GENERAL VONGUYEN GIAP – NORTH VIETNAMESE GENERAL

I HAVE WRITTEN about how the politicians intervened in the Vietnam War causing the military to not win when they could have won. Part of the problem was the negative press from the news media that shaped the political attitude of the politicians along with the demonstrations and rioting of war dissenters. Votes and political donations rule the politicians. These are the words of an important North Vietnamese General, General VoNguyen Giap.

General Giap was a brilliant, highly respected leader in the North Vietnam military. The following quote is from his memoirs currently found in the Vietnam war memorial in Hanoi: "What we still don't understand is why you Americans stopped the bombing of Hanoi. You had us on the ropes. If you had pressed us a little harder, just for another day or two, we were ready to surrender. It was the same in the Battle of TET. You defeated us! We knew it, and we thought you knew it! But we were elated to notice your media was helping us. They were causing more disruption in America than we could in the battlefields. We were ready to surrender. You had won!"

General Giap has published his memoirs and confirmed what most Americans knew. The U.S. military did not understand

Vietnam and guerilla warfare. The sentiment that the U.S. lost the war at home because of anti-war protests and news media coverage actually came from Bui Tin, a former colonel in the North Vietnamese Army, during a 1995 interview with the Wall Street Journal. When asked about the anti-war movement's impact on the war, Tin replied. "It was essential to our strategy. Support of the war from our rear was completely secure while the American rear was vulnerable. Every day our leadership would listen to the world news over the radio at 9 a.m. to follow the growth of the American anti-war movement. We were elated when Jane Fonda visited Hanoi and later, wearing a red Vietnamese dress, said at a press conference that she was ashamed of American actions in the war and that she would struggle along with us." Anti-war protesters and the news media failed to support patriotic and freedom loving Vietnam soldiers and our war effort.

THE VIETNAM WAR STILL RAGING FOR VIETNAM VETERANS 40 YEARS LATER

THE VIETNAM WAR is not over 40 years later for Vietnam veterans. It is time to talk about that part of the Vietnam War. Most Americans have heard about Agent Orange, but they do not know much about it. It is time to learn. Some of the information in this Vietnam story has come from an article on Agent Orange printed in the New York Times. From 1962 to 1971, American C-123 transport planes sprayed roughly 20 million gallons of herbicides on an area of South Vietnam about the size of Massachusetts. Code-named "Ranch Hand," this operation reached its peak from 1967 to 1969. [Some members of the Ranch Hand team adopted Smokey Bear (of forest-fire awareness fame) as a mascot. "Only you can prevent a forest" was their twist on Smokey's slogan.]

The purpose of using Agent Orange was to destroy the thick jungle so the North Vietnamese Army and the Viet Cong could not hide in it and to make them ill. An exposed enemy soldier or an ill enemy soldier eventually became a dead enemy soldier!

To the political and military strategists in Washington, DC, using vegetation-killing chemicals was a legally sound and necessary way to save American and South Vietnamese lives. Naturally, money and politics influenced this decision. News outlets have returned to examine vegetation spraying in Vietnam and to the chemical most commonly and most notoriously used there: Agent Orange. Named for the color of a stripe girding the barrels in which it was shipped, it combined two herbicides, one of which turned out to be contaminated with a highly toxic strain of dioxin. No need for alarm, Washington, DC officialdom and chemical company executives insisted at the time (money and politics), Agent Orange did not harm humans, they said.

As the late 1960s wore on, those assurances increasingly rang hollow. Researchers found evidence of birth defects in lab animals. American scientists and others began to speak out against the spraying. Opposition to the herbicide campaign mounted, arm in arm with protests spreading against the war. In 1970, the Agent Orange spraying stopped. Other chemicals continued to be used until Jan. 7, 1971, when the entire herbicide program was scrapped after a final "Ranch Hand" run.

Here at home, the war has not ended for many of the 2.8 million servicemen and women who went to Vietnam. These ailing veterans are convinced that their cancers and nervous disorders and skin diseases (not to mention congenital maladies afflicting some of their children) are a result of their contact with Agent Orange. Often enough, that linkage has not been established incontrovertibly. Studies on Agent Orange's effects tend to use language that is less than absolute. Certain illnesses, for instance, are said to be "associated" with dioxin exposure. Or there is a "presumptive" connection. That said, the American government's resistance to connecting the dots in any manner has melted away over the years. The Agent Orange Act of 1991 accepted a presumed link to illnesses like non-Hodgkin's lymphoma, soft-tissue sarcoma and chloracne. Veterans with those ailments were declared eligible for medical treatment and financial compensation without having to prove they had been exposed to herbicides. It is assumed if you were in the Vietnam War, you were exposed to Agent Orange and the years of residue it left behind.

Over time, more than a dozen other maladies, including Hodgkin's disease and prostate cancer, were steadily added to this list. Type 2 diabetes has been added as well as some nervous disorders and birth defects in children of Vietnam veterans. The spraying of Agent Orange stopped prior to my arriving in Vietnam, but they used other vegetation killers not as dangerous health-wise as Agent Orange. However, the residue of Agent Orange lingers for years. Being a Crew Chief/Gunner on a Scout LOACH, flying missions as a Hunter/Killer Team, rotor wash from our helicopters stirred up the residue of Agent Orange. I am presently being treated for Agent Orange by VA and receiving VA Disability Benefits. The effects of Agent Orange on my body are under control to the point I enjoy a full and healthy life. I wonder if that would be the case if VA was not treating me and thousands of other Vietnam Veterans for Agent Orange.

Since the Federal Government did not recognize Agent Orange as a health hazard until 1991, many Vietnam Veterans contracted diseases related to Agent Orange and died before they could receive preventative or healing treatment or medicine. Since our politicians were responsible for Agent Orange being used in Vietnam, they are trying to ease their guilty feelings by giving disability to Vietnam War veterans and their families. I am grateful they are feeling guilty!

The people of Vietnam are not so fortunate. They do not have the medical care we have. They have been suffering with birth defects in their children and physical effects for years! The United States government has finally bellied up and is eliminating the biggest problem areas, the areas called "hot spots," where the Agent Orange was stored. They do this by burning the areas with fires that heat up to 600 degrees. That immense heat destroys the dangerous parts of the herbicide. I am grateful the Federal Government has accepted the responsibility of so many sick veterans and providing the medical care they need. I feel all the side effects affecting Vietnam veterans being social problems, health problems, and psychological problems caused by war and not receiving any welcome home at all by the general public, is being rectified. I feel much better about my service in Vietnam! I know many of my Vietnam brothers feel the same! I can say now, "I am proud to have fought in Vietnam." I could never ever say that until here recently. Thank you, America! We never, ever stopped loving you! (Information in this story about agent orange was taken from the websites History.com and Wikipedia.)

Vietnam - Barrel of Agent Orange

Vietnam - Ranch Hand Run Spraying Agent Orange

VIETNAM - WHEN I JUST ABOUT BECAME A POW (PRISONER OF WAR)

IT IS IMPORTANT for families to know their history. So many family historical events leave this earth unknown. I am sharing my Vietnam stories to keep that from happening in my family. When the 4th Division was sent back to the United States after occupying An Khe, South Vietnam for several years, the base camp was turned over to the Vietnamese, except for the air strip and some buildings around it. We used the An Khe air strip as the base for all of our missions. Our company was attached to another Division that had us move to An Thon, about a half hour helicopter flight from An Khe. We made that half hour flight each day before going out on a mission. There was always a Hunter/Killer Team that stayed in An Khe at night and flew back to An Thon the next morning. That is where I finished up the last few months of my year and half tour in Vietnam.

Our base camp was near the village of An Thon. The village was off limits to all American soldiers for security and safety reasons. As I have mentioned in other stories, the stress was exceedingly high for all soldiers in Vietnam. That is why the military gave soldiers two R&R's (Rest and Recuperation) for the year they served there. If a soldier served more than a year in Vietnam, they received more R&R's. However, for me, I needed a little more rest and recuperation than that. I would sneak out through our perimeter wire around 10 A.M. in the morning, go down to the village, stay all night, and come back through the wire at 10 a.m. the next morning. I always went through the wire at a guard tower where I knew the person who was on guard duty at that tower. We would wave at each other as I went by. They always watched me come back with a smile on my face the next morning. I had gotten to be friends with Mama-son (older Vietnamese woman). The Viet Cong had killed her husband and taken her sons away to be enemy soldiers. Mama-son really liked me. She was always thrilled to see me come to visit. She loved to make egg rolls for me, because she made the best egg rolls ever eaten and I let her know it. Number One, Mama-son! Number One, Mama-son! She would smile at me with her "missing teeth smile" and just glow with pride. I could not come back through the perimeter wire at our base camp compound at night, because I would be shot! Not the kind of shot I was looking for. I would stay all night sleeping in a hammock outside Mama-son's hooch. I was sitting outside one evening while visiting with Mama-son as she was making me some egg rolls. All of a sudden, ten Viet Cong soldiers appeared, armed to the teeth. My heart jumped into my throat! I thought, Oh! Crap! I am going to become a prisoner of war (POW). Luckily, I was smart enough not to wear a shirt that had my Scout patch on it. There was a $1000 reward for the capture or killing of anyone wearing that patch. I sat there on pins and needles. I always left my weapons back at the compound.

The Viet Cong each helped themselves to Mama-son's egg rolls (the ones she was making for me), chatted with each other, then headed out as quickly as they appeared. They were on their way to attack one of our base camps, but not ours. They completely ignored me. They did not want me to burden them on their mission, which was still quite far away. I checked to make sure I had not crapped my pants. That was the most scared I had ever been in Vietnam at that time. Mama-son told me that every so often a patrol of Viet Cong would come through to stop and eat something. I did not sleep that night at all. All I could do was wait impatiently for daylight so I could go back to my own bed! I realized then why the upper brass made the village off limits.

Mama-son did not see me for a while after that little incident. She laughed and called me "Ga" which means "chicken or fowl" in Vietnamese. I would have fun with her, walking around like a chicken, flapping my arms, and clucking like a chicken. She said I was "gan" which means "batty" or "loco" in Vietnamese. So much for rest and recuperation!

Vietnam - Civilian Village Hooch (house)

Vietnamese Egg Roll

Map of South Vietnam

VIETNAM – HANOI JANE, A TRAITOR

VIETNAM VETERANS ALWAYS come to my mind whenever I have appointments at the VA Clinic. My heart aches for them! I always wonder what the Vietnam War was like for them. Does the pain ever die? Maybe for some, but for most no.

I am one that does not want to hate. Hate is a very destructive emotion that affects the hater so greatly. Most of the time the one hated does not even know it. The one hate I am still struggling with is the hatred I have had for the actress Jane Fonda! Hanoi Jane! I, to this day, will not watch any of her movies or TV shows. When she was nominated for a "Woman of the Year" award not too long ago, that hatred pot was stirred up again! My Vietnam brothers were stirred up also! It is hard to forget what she did public relations (PR) wise for the North Vietnamese and the untrue propaganda she spread about how well our prisoners of war were being treated. For her to have the gall to visit with the North Vietnamese while we were at war is reprehensible! She has made public statements the last few years she wished she would not have done those things, but she has never made an acceptable apology to the Vietnam veterans. I know that forgiveness is a Christ-like attribute. I hope and pray I can live up to the miracle of forgiveness! Jane Fonda is making it very, very difficult!

VIETNAM - THE EMOTIONS OF ARRIVING HOME COMING FROM THE VIETNAM WAR

I HAVE MENTIONED in other stories that I made a pact with myself that I was coming home alive and in one piece. Many of my Vietnam brothers did not have that blessing. I did. When I became a short timer (not much time left in Vietnam), I decided to quit flying on missions thirty days before I returned home to the "World" (the United States). I did not want to take a chance of not making it home. Many, many times soldiers went on missions just a day or two before they were to go home and did not make it. I was not going to tempt the grim reaper! I laid around sleeping, reading, talking with my buddy's, helping out at the maintenance hangar, and running around our base camp compound to keep in shape. I had quit smoking while in Vietnam. I started smoking six years earlier. I needed to get my wind back.

My endurance was important to me. Then came the day to fly out to Cam Ranh Bay to be processed out to go home. I do not remember being so anxious in my whole life. We processed through, were bused to a holding area, and waited, and waited, and waited! Finally, the time came to board our plane home for the 18-hour flight home. I could not sleep a wink. I was thinking so much what it had been like at home before I was drafted, thinking about my friends, the girls I dated, and about my family. We landed at Ft McCord Air Force Base just outside of Seattle/Tacoma Washington area. It was an outside deplaning situation. When I got to the bottom of the steps of the stairs to the airplane passenger door, I stopped, got down on my knees, and kissed the ground. How sweet it was to kiss the United States of America! Most of us on that plane did it. What an emotional time!

We were bused to our temporary barracks at Ft. Lewis, Washington to finish processing out. I was being discharged from the Army. I had extended six months on my Vietnam tour so I would get an early out. I had extended for a year at Basic Training to get a special six months training school and fast rank (I needed the money) so I would not become a grunt (infantryman). In addition to my two years from being drafted, I had to give another year. I hated state side duty. It was boring. I was always a very hard worker being raised on a ranch in South Dakota. The military will make one very lazy very quickly. I do not mean to say there are not some hard-working military people. I just did not see any of that during my state side duty prior to being shipped to Vietnam. As I mentioned in an earlier story, I was addicted to adrenaline. I wanted to feed my addiction for as long as I possibly could. So, I extended for six months for combat duty.

This entitled me to a six month early out. It was early December 1971 when I boarded the plane for Custer, South Dakota. None of my family knew I was coming home. My plane landed in Rapid City, South Dakota and I hired a cab to drive me the fifty miles to Custer. I decided I needed a beer before I went home. My Dad, my stepmother, my oldest sister, Bernadine, and my youngest sister, Lois still lived at home on the outskirts of Custer on our 400-acre ranch that had the most beautiful valley one can ever enjoy. I had the cab driver drop me off on Main Street in Custer at a beer and pool place across the street from the drug store. I am getting out of the cab and unloading my duffel bag out of the trunk, I hear this screaming of my name, "R-a-n-d-y!!!" It was my oldest sister, Bernadine. Unbeknownst to me she worked at the drug store after school. We hugged, kissed, and I swung her around off her feet! It was pure joy! Bernadine informed me that Dad was picking her up at five o'clock after he got off work at the sawmill. I told her not to tell Dad I was there, but to come get me when he came. I played some pool and drank some beer. Finally, Bernadine came to the door of the pub to inform me Dad was there to pick her up. I grabbed my duffel bag and proceeded out the door. Then my Dad saw me. We rushed into each other's arms in the middle of Main Street in Custer, South Dakota both of us crying. I whispered in my Dad's ear saying, "Dad! It was a real bitch!" I then picked up my duffel bag, threw it into the back of Dad's pickup, and we drove home.

The emotions poured out all over again, as I had a group hug with my step mother and youngest sister, Lois. My step mother told me later it had been many years since she had that good of a cry. Me! I still can't keep from crying. I am a tough, hard sucker on the outside, but inside I have a tender heart. That is a Tompkins trait. As days passed by, I tried to work my way back into a normal life pattern. But no one really wanted anything to do with me. My friends abandoned me. Nothing was what I had dreamed it was going to be like when I arrived home. It hurt! It hurt so much I left and moved to Minneapolis, Minnesota. I knew then I would never be able to share anything about my

Vietnam experiences. America did not want to listen. I was a "woman and a baby killer!" I really was not a monster! I was only a young man that needed love and understanding. The only thing I got was, "Get the hell out of Dodge! Ride off into the sunset! Don't come back!"

That is all in the past. Writing stories of my Vietnam stories is like washing the dirty clothes. Each time I wrote one the cleaner my soul has become. I want to thank my God for all the strength and blessings He had given me to help me cope with the hidden pain until I could see fit to take the cap off the pain container and let it all out! Never in a million years did I ever think writing these stories would do that. It has helped me far, far beyond my expectations. I am now proud to say I served in Vietnam. America wants to wrap their arms around all us and finally say, "Welcome home, Heroes!"

All I have to say to my Vietnam War brothers is, "I love you guys. I see your pain. I feel your agony. I promise you that will all go away if you choose to write your Vietnam War experiences from the heart on paper or by recording them. The light is beautiful at the end of the journey! "I say Biet!" (goodbye in Vietnamese).

Freedom Bird (plane) Landing In "The World" (United States)

Emotional Reunion With Vietnam War Returnee's Family

SOMETHING I DISCOVERED ABOUT AMERICA AND VIETNAM VETERANS

IN THE PROCESS of writing this book on my Vietnam War experiences through all this process that started August 14, 2018, I have learned my stories are helping a lot of Vietnam War veterans. These guys are my brothers. The gals are my sisters. I want to help them all I can. Vietnam veterans need a lot of healing from years of suffering as a result of our war experiences and the way we were all treated when we arrived home. It was terrible! It was painful! It was not right!

Many of my brothers have been suffering for too many years. I am trying to help them come out of the Vietnam War closet to be healed. Writing 35 stories that I sent to family and posted on Facebook was responsible for my healing. I am now proud to say that I served in the Vietnam War. There was a lot of pain, loneliness, fear, sorrow, discomfort, hate, bitching, complaining, crying, and home sickness that we all have had to deal with. This process has helped me overcome all of that.

America hated us. This was brought about by a biased news media, protests by anti-war protesters, gutless politicians, and a scared America.

What do I mean by a scared America? Right now, I sincerely

believe America wants to repent of the way Vietnam Veterans were treated when they arrived home. I have been the recipient of this repentance. I have received hundreds of "thank you for your service" and "I love you" since August 14, 2018.

There is one thing I finally figured out as I have been writing my book and reading other books written by Vietnam War veterans in preparation for writing my book. Our fellow Americans were scared of us. I do not really blame them. My oldest sister, Bernadine, said all I did was pace around the house when I arrived home from Vietnam. I do not even remember that or realized I was doing it. She thought I was on some-kind-of-a-drug. After reading my stories, she finally realized I was withdrawing from being addicted to adrenaline. She is right. I was addicted to adrenaline. Adrenaline is very addictive.

After focusing on killing the enemy for one and half years in Vietnam, I probably came across as a monster. My friends and community members did not know how to deal with it. So, they just shunned me. I left town. Piss on them, I thought (I realized later why I did not understand).

In talking with many other Vietnam Veterans, they experienced the same thing. Since we did not understand or know how to deal with the problem, we buried our feelings deep in a place where the pain could be numbed.

I am very sorry I never understood how my friends and community felt. I am very sorry for all my anger towards them and blaming them. I wish I would have been stronger spiritually and in tune enough to have made it a much better experience helping others to understand. I realize now I have as much repenting to do as America. I am so sorry! I have a suggestion. Why don't we all have a big group hug (mentally)? Hug-Hug-Hug! Damn that felt good! I am now a very, very proud Vietnam War veteran.

ABOUT THE AUTHOR

Randall (Randy) Leonard Tompkins (nick named Peewee growing up) was born in Pierre, South Dakota to Leo Jacob Tompkins and Violet (Vi) March Pratt July 2, 1946. He lived on a farm with his family five miles east of Highmore, South Dakota until the end of his sixth-grade year at age 11. At age 10 his mother, Vi, died from complications in surgery at the age of 37. That left his father, Leo, to finish raising six children. Larry 13 years old. Randy 10 years old, Bernard (Bernie) 8 years old, James (Mutt) 4 years old, Bernadine (Sis) 2 years old, and Lois three months old.

The family sold the almost 1000-acre farm at Highmore and moved to Timber Lake, South Dakota to purchase and lease 3000-acres of ranch land 10 miles south of Timber Lake in June 1958.

Randy graduated in May 1964 from Timber Lake High School. November 1963 the ranch was sold. The family moved to Custer, South Dakota purchasing a 400-acre ranch just on the west side of Custer. Randy stayed with a neighbor in Timber Lake to finish up his senior year in high school. After graduation, he moved to Custer.

Randy was drafted May 29, 1969 while working in the oil fields of Wyoming after working the prior two logging seasons in Alaska. He returned home to Custer, South Dakota after serving in the Vietnam War December 10, 1971.

Randy has been married to Sally Arlene Best for 45 years. They have two grown children and a grown granddaughter. Randy retired as a real estate broker in Zanesville, Ohio in 2008. He started a small construction and maintenance company later. He and Sally still reside in Zanesville, Ohio.

ACKNOWLEDGMENTS

I want to take this time to thank all of you who have encouraged me to write this book. Your encouragement and love through out this whole process has been uplifting and filled with gratitude. I want to specifically thank my proof readers Adele Enright, Pat Kjellsen, Carol Coakwell, Larry Tompkins, and Kathy Nelson, publisher of the Timber Lake Topic. I cannot place a value on what their help has meant. I will forever be indebted to them.

I also want to thank all of my Facebook friends, Timber Lake High School schoolmates I went to school with, people who live in or have connections to the Timber Lake, South Dakota area, and all the Vietnam War veterans who have cheered me on.

None of this would have ever happened if my brothers and sisters had not gotten angry with me for not sharing my Vietnam War experiences with them, especially my youngest sister, Lois. They have gotten to know a side of me they never knew. I love them dearly. They are a strength to me body and soul. My values and character are intertwined with theirs.

Of course, I want to thank my dear wife, Sally, who has been by my side through all of this. She is my eternal mate! Her love helps me to have the joy I have in life.

I also want to thank my Savior Jesus Christ and my Heavenly Father for all my many blessings. My harvest is bountiful. I am blessed. Thank you.

CONTACT INFORMATION

Randy Tompkins
3500 Foxfire Drive
Zanesville OH 43701
740-819-1872 (cell phone)
stompkin@columbus.rr.com (email address)

Please feel free to contact me with your comments!

CPSIA information can be obtained
at www.ICGtesting.com
Printed in the USA
BVHW091933270519
549385BV00004B/6/P